Above and Below the Limestone

The Pits and People of Easington District

David Temple

Printed and published by TUPS Books in partnership with The District of Easington

TUPS Books, 30 Lime Street, Newcastle upon Tyne, NE1 2PQ
Tel No: 0191 2330990 Fax: 0191 2330578

Soft back ISBN 1-901237-20-6
Hard back ISBN 1-901237-21-4

Foreword

It gives me great pleasure to welcome you to another milestone in the District of Easington's publishing history.

Above and Below the Limestone graphically portrays the history of the District's mining settlements and the contribution these places and more importantly the people have made to British history.

Britain in the 21st century has been shaped by the working-class struggle which tried to keep social reform in pace with the great technological reforms that started to radically change the face of Britain in the Industrial Revolution.

Our Institutions, Government and social mores have all been shaped by this struggle, and the District's settlements all contributed to this history in the making.

As we go forward into a new century with its new opportunities and challenges it is important for us to understand our history and roots as this can positively effect the decisions of today which will shape the actions of tomorrow.

Dave Temple's mixture of society and science, well researched and accessibly written, gives us that history. As you read this book, you will gain an in-depth insight into our mining past and perhaps you will want to come and visit the District to enjoy our post-mining renewal and share with us our hopes and plans for the future

Councillor WR Peardon
Chairman of the District of Easington

This book is dedicated to the memory of Marjorie and Jack 'Shacky' Taylor, two fine examples of all that is best in the people of Easington District

Acknowledgements

Above and Below the Limestone would not have been possible without the foresight of John Cummings MP when he was leader of Easington District Council. He saw the importance of collecting and preserving the memories of members of the community in a series of interviews. As a result Bob Porter of Peterlee was instrumental executing a programme of tape recordings, in the 1970s and early 1980s, which now constitute an invaluable archive. The programme also included the collection of old photographs which make up what must be one of the finest photographic archives held by any District Council.

I would like to thank Adam Sutherland, Senior Cultural Development Officer of the District of Easington and all the staff of the Cultural Development Department for their friendly and good-natured co-operation. Also Barry Chambers, former secretary of Blackhall colliery NUM lodge, for his help and encouragement, Louise Fenwick for the design of the front cover, and illustrator Ann Wood for her illustrations on pages 10 and 33.

Index

Introduction

It is 15,000 years since the great glaciers retreated from the North of England. Like landscape gardeners they had put the finishing touches to the countryside we recognise today. Just as the bulldozers have flattened the pit heaps that dominated East Durham for 150 years the glaciers of the ice age smoothed the contours of a rough-hewn landscape.

But this was recent history. The process that gave life to the towns and villages of East Durham began 300 million years ago in tropical forests and swamps. The human brain cannot comprehend the almost infinite time in which nature laid down the coal measures of the Great Northern Coalfield, no more than it can comprehend the billions upon billions of sea creatures that lived and died, each one contributing a minuscule fraction to the great limestone cap of East Durham.

After the ice plant life returned with a speed that only nature can achieve. First the lichens and mosses, then the grasses and finally the forest. A barren, inert landscape to the thriving oak and beech forests took only a thousand or so years for nature to achieve. Man took a little longer to chop it all down. And when it was all but gone, all used up on the timber-framed houses, the smithies' fires and the keels of great trading ships, a substitute had to be found. But the substitute was already there.

Coal had been used in the North East of England from the beginning of the first millennium. Coal first exposed itself on the river banks. From these outcrops it beckoned challenging man to follow it into its subterranean world, into a world full of danger, of rich rewards and great disappointments. Nature had created a complicated and dangerous puzzle for man to solve. A seam of coal could be of exceptional quality, thick and easy to win and then it would disappear, leaving a solid face of stone, neatly separated from the coal as if cut by some precision tool. A good strong sandstone roof may without notice change to a soft clay, like shale incapable of support. Man had to lean to read the signs and map this three-dimensional darkness.

To lighten the darkness the first miners had only

one tool, nurtured since the primeval days - the light of burning tinder. Nature replied with firedamp, methane gas, that seeped from the coal seams and when mixed with air only required a spark to create an explosion of devastating force. Sometimes firedamp was present in great abundance; sometimes it was hardly perceptible, but it was always unpredictable.

The coal created a new breed of man, a new kind of community and a new culture. Coal created a huge industry that was to force the pace of engineering innovation and change the world.

For over three centuries, the growing demand for energy was satisfied by Durham's accessible coal measures in the west, in the broad valley of the Wear and on the steep banks of the Tyne. But as the shallow drifts became exhausted, pits were sunk deeper, and still deeper and further away from the rivers. When nature's geology won the battle for the coal, and it frequently did, these new pits were abandoned and still more were sunk.

The struggle to win coal forced mankind to harness the very power of the coal itself, and transform it into a greater power, the power of steam. Steam power had been used as early as 1729, when Thomas Newcomen invented a crude steam engine to pump water out of Cornish tin mines. His engine, however, was inefficient and could only produce straight-line motion. James Watt increased its efficiency in 1781, and with the use of a crankshaft transformed the linear motion into circular motion. At the beginning of the eighteenth century new and more efficient steam engines kick-started the manic development of the Industrial Revolution. The speed of development was breathtaking. By 1815 the first crude locomotives of Stephenson and Hackworth were linking the pits of the Great Northern Coalfield. Two decades later railways were pushing out into the Russian Steppes and the North American Prairies. The battle for coal had developed steam power. Now the world demanded this new power in ever increasing quantities.

The process of providing this power did not run smoothly. Supply and demand were always out of phase. Boom and bust, stop and go, created good times and bad times and intensified the conflict between master and men. This economic roller-coaster essentially formed the character of the people of Durham and their communities. Unions, Cooperatives, education, self-help and solidarity were all fashioned on the anvil of hardship as mining communities were squeezed between the downturn in trade and the profit margins of the masters.

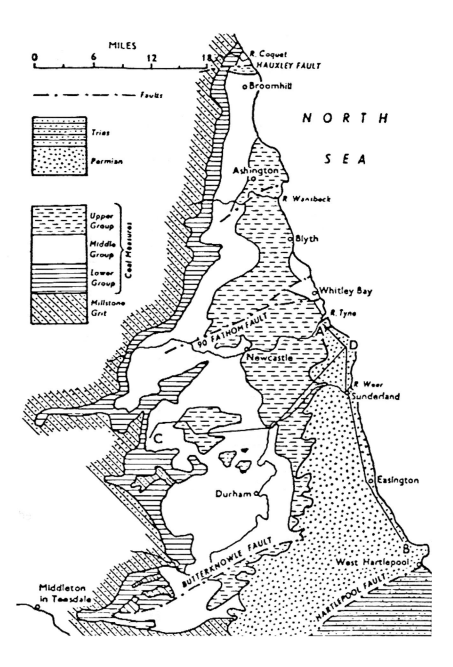

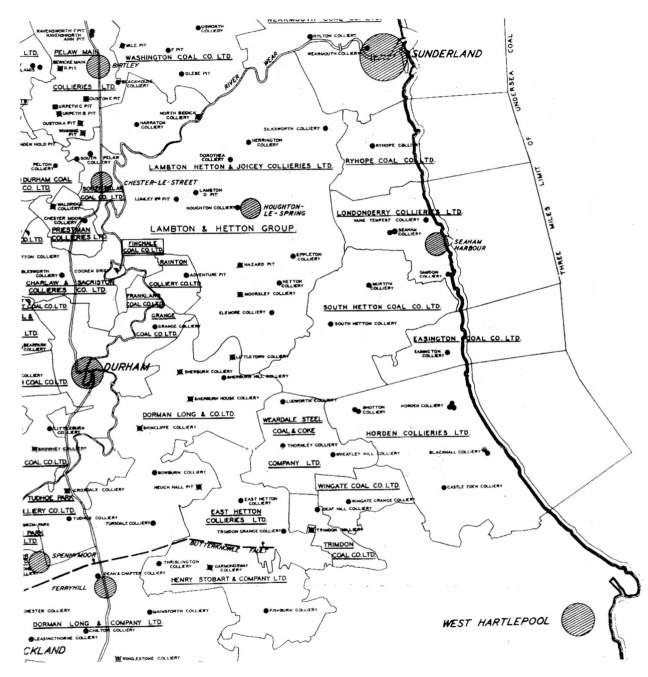

Chapter 1

Hetton colliery , sketch by TH Hair

Coal mining in Durham was already many centuries old before it came to the Easington area. The eighteenth century had left this corner of Durham unspoiled by the ravages of mining. Its windswept limestone and boulder clay cliffs, its undulating, fertile and well drained soil, remained much as they had been for centuries. The limestone escarpment of East Durham was a bracing and pleasing place to live but none got very rich from its soil. When the southern counties feel the first warming rays of the spring sun, East Durham is still braving the chilling eastern gales that delay the growing season by a month or more.

As the eighteenth century closed the squires and tenant farmers of East Durham looked out enviously over the mid-Durham plain at the rapidly advancing pit-heads. The question they asked and the one question which dominated the coalfield was: just how extensive were Durham's coal reserves? Geologists had long believed that the coal seams of mid-Durham disappeared on western edge of the limestone, but no one could be certain.

A mining engineer called Beaumont invented bore rods as early as 1620. This allowed prospectors to determine the position and quality of underground seams without the costly expense of sinking shafts or drifting large distances from outcrops. But this technology had its limitations The limestone cap of East Durham was itself on average 350 ft. deep and contained no workable coal. The seams of mid-Durham dipped to the east and the question geologists asked was: if coal measures extended under the limestone, how far would they continue to dip? 1,000 ft. or perhaps 2,000 ft.? This was well out of the reach of the drill rods of the day, which had only managed to reach a depth of about 700 ft and it was deeper,

far deeper, than any pit had ever been sunk. Would the coal be of the same quality or would the whole operation be just one big expensive flop? It was a gamble. But mining was a gamble. Miners gamble with their lives, but whoever was to go beyond the limestone was going to gamble big money. This was to be the gamble of the century! Too big a gamble even for the big landowning aristocrats who had hitherto dominated Durham's coal trade.

Commercial adventurers had long before devised a method of spreading the risk of such gambles, and this was known as the joint stock company. A number of partners would pool their capital in order to invest it in a commercial venture.

The first attempt to sink a shaft through the limestone was made in 1810 by William Lyons on his estate in Hetton. He did not prove the existence of coal beneath the limestone but he did prove that once again nature had laid a trap. Immediately beneath the limestone was a bed of water and sand up to 60ft in depth that constituted a lethal barrier. As soon as his shaft reached this bed the shaft became inundated with water and the whole project was abandoned. Lyons may well have been the last man to attempt to penetrate the limestone, but for the faith of an eminent geologist, Dr William Smith.

William Smith was rightly hailed as the 'Father

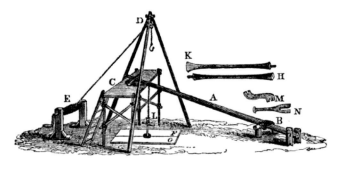

Early boring tools

of English Geology'. He made the first scientific survey and produced the first geological map of England. He became known by the less grand title of 'Strata Smith', due to his habit of lecturing, to anyone who would listen, about geological strata.

The conventional wisdom amongst the foremost mining engineers in Newcastle decreed that no coal could possibly exist below magnesium limestone and if it did it would be of such inferior quality as not to be worth mining. Smith, however, made a detailed study of the strata as it approached the limestone escarpment and predicted that coal existed at depths that could be reached by the mining techniques of the day. He predicted that the best place to reach this coal was at the village of Haswell.

In 1811 he was instrumental in sinking a shaft at Haswell, which was successful in reaching coal. The success was however short-lived, as the pressure of the water in the sand feeder eventually forced its way into the shaft and the shaft was abandoned, leaving the coal company £60,000 the poorer. Now there was no doubt that coal existed below the limestone, but the failure of Smith and Lyons to solve the problem of the sand feeder delayed any further attempts at a sinking for a decade.

It was however only a matter of time before the promise of such riches would attract the attention

Sinkers at work

of men with sufficient capital and courage to face the sand feeder. In 1821 the Hetton Coal company amassed £60,000 to sink the Hetton Lyons Blossom pit, on what they considered was a six-to-one shot which would net them a cool £360,000 during the lifetime of the pit. In so doing they created the first deep pit in the world and proved that coal measures of good quality lay beneath the limestone. Sinking a shaft through limestone is a relatively easy task, through the pressurised waters of the sand feeder it was perilous.

The engineers who began this sinking did so without the benefit of steel. In 1821 iron was either cast or wrought, and it was weaker than steel. The power that could be transmitted from a steam engine was limited by the weight and strength of the cranks and connecting rods.

Pumps were made of wooden segments, bound by iron hoops to form a barrel-like tube. Inside the tube a wooden piston attached to the beam of a steam engine oscillated vertically, lifting the water and ejecting it through a crude non-return valve consisting of a leather flap, called a bucket.

There was a limit to the height of water that could be supported by the piston, and water had to be taken up the shaft in a series of lifts. One pump would fill into a large cast iron tank while a second

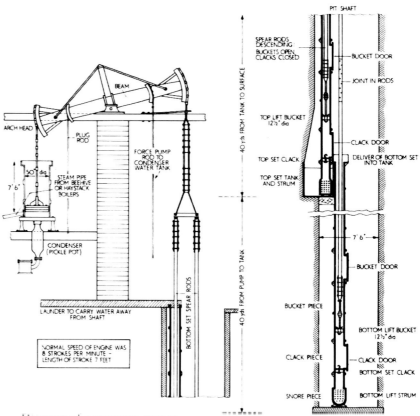

Diagram of a pumping engine

would pump this water out of the tank to the next tank further up the shaft. This was in itself a laborious business, but the sinkers had a further problem to contend with. The mixture of sand and water in the sand feeder quickly wore away the leather flaps of the buckets, which had to be replaced on an almost daily basis.

These crude pumps had to be arranged in such

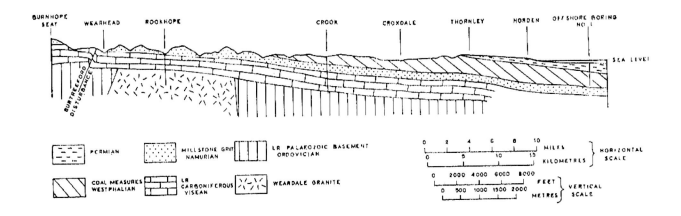

numbers that they held the water at bay while the shaft sides were sealed. The sealing of the shaft was called 'tubbing'. Curved cast iron sections were forced against the sides of the shaft by a mechanism known as a 'wedging-crib' and bolted together. The gaps between the sections were then water-proofed by hammering lead into the gaps, much as the plates of a riveted ship were corked. By this method the Hetton sinkers were able to win the battle against the sand feeder, which was pouring into the shaft at a rate of 5,000 gallons a minute.

Once it had been proved that the limestone and the sand feeder could be penetrated, the race was on. The Hetton Coal Company had the advantage of experience and resources and was quick to sink two more shafts close to the Blossom in the Hetton area, and in 1825 began the sinking of Ellemore colliery, between Easington Lane and at Hetton on the Hill, and Eppleton colliery on Hetton Downs.

In 1831 Colonel Braddylle sank South Hetton pit successfully. But he came unstuck when he attempted a new sinking at Murton. This legendary battle against the sand feeder ended with Colonel Braddylle in bankruptcy court, and gave rise to the South Hetton Coal Company; living proof that in mining as in all games of chance there are both winners and losers.
The old Durham aristocracy was affronted by this intrusion into its monopoly but was testimony to the old adage : if you cant beat them, join them.

In 1827 the Earl of Durham, Lord Lambton, entered the fray and sunk Houghton colliery, and later bought into the Hetton Coal Company to form the Lambton and Hetton Group.

Now the question was posed: now that it had been proved that the coal measures continued beneath the limestone where would they end? Would they peter out on the cliff tops or would they extend out to sea. Messrs Thompson Pemberton and Co. were determined to gamble again and for higher stakes. In 1835 they risked a small fortune in the sinking of Wearmouth colliery, which then became the deepest mine in the world, finally reaching the Harvey seam at a depth of 1852 ft.

Seaham

The coastal strip from Seaham southward remained as it had been for a millennium: barren, windswept and in the main devoid of population. In 1810 Seaham boasted a population of 22 persons, by 1811 there were 27, and by 1821 35. But all was to change — changed by one man, Lord Stewart, a soldier from a relatively poor Anglo-Irish family. Although not wealthy he had friends in high places and counted the Duke of Wellington, with whom he had fought at the Battle of Waterloo in 1815, as one of them. His half-brother was Lord Castlereagh, a leading Minister in the Government of George 111. Stewart was to raise himself out of his relative poverty in the only

way open to such aristocrats: by making a good marriage. His chosen bride was the lovely, famously wealthy 19-year-old heiress, Lady Frances Ann Vane Tempest. Lady Frances was a ward of court and heir to her family's collieries in mid-Durham. The marriage was not without opposition from her relatives, who did all in their power to prevent Lord Stewart getting his hands on the family fortune. However, despite their protestations Charles William Stewart married Lady Frances in 1819, and when his half-brother Lord Castlereagh died in 1822 Stewart assumed the title of The Third Marquis of Londonderry, a name that was to dominate Durham and particularly East Durham for well over 100 years.

By 1819 the rapid expansion of the coalfield to meet the needs of the Industrial Revolution created problems of transporting such huge volumes of coal. Londonderry's collieries at Rainton and Pittington produced 250,000 tons of coal per year, carried overland to the staithes at Penshaw where they were loaded into keels and taken to Sunderland.

Once on the Wear, Londonderry's coal had to compete with that of the other owners. The river was highly congested and cargoes were often delayed for weeks. Londonderry estimated that he was paying £10,000 per year to the River Wear for the privilege. His solution was to avoid both the congestion and the cost by the construction of an artificial harbour close to the hamlet of Seaham, and to connect this new harbour to his pits by rail.

Londonderry acquired the land for the new harbour from Sir Ralph Millbanke. Millibanke's daughter Anna Isabella had fallen in love with the wayward poet Lord Byron. It is difficult to know exactly if the feelings were mutual but contemporary opinion seams to suggest that Byron was more interested in the £20,000 dowry that Millbanke was to pay him. To raise this enormous sum he mortgaged his estate and in 1815 Byron and Nancy married. The marriage did not last and Byron absconded abroad to avoid the disapproval of society.

Milbanke auctioned the land in 1821 and it was snapped up by Londonderry. Londonderry was short of capital. Much of his wife's money was in a trust fund beyond his reach and the trustees would not release finance for what they considered a risky venture. Londonderry had to borrow heavily from London bankers and it was not until 1828 that the first stone of the harbour wall was laid. The inner harbour was completed in 1831. The population of Seaham had by now risen to 1,033.

We can picture the scene. On the once deserted

The coal drops at Sunderland, sketch by TH Hair

cliff tops a new community was taking shape. New stone-built rows of cottages, not yet disfigured by the grime of an industrial town, overlooked colliers in the new harbour. Children born in different villages and towns of Durham played excitedly in the streets. Sailors drank, gambled and fought. Durham dialects with their subtle differences could be heard alongside those of the Irish and Scottish immigrants. Everyone was a stranger in this new town. No one yet belonged.

A continuous line of chaldron wagons clanked and squealed down to the docks past the Irish quarter. A new workshops and a bottle factory were already built. As yet there were no coal mines in Seaham, but this was soon to change.

While Londonderry was completing his new harbour at Seaham the coalfield was in turmoil.

The sinking of the Hetton colliery in 1820 had attracted a young 27-year-old hewer by the name of Thomas Hepburn. In 1822 he converted to the Primitive Methodist calling and became a lay preacher. This particular virulent sect of the Methodists was strongly pro-union, and after the repeal of the Combination Acts in 1825 Hepburn and his co-thinkers had formed a new, legal trade union, replacing the illegal Brotherhood which had previously existed. This new union was called The Colliers of the United Association of Durham and Northumberland.

Pitmen strike

By 1831 the overwhelming majority of pitmen in the two counties had united in the new union and they refused to accept the terms of the 1831 bond. When the pitmen refused to bind themselves the owners' committee locked the pitmen out and began to evict them from their colliery houses. This action could not have come at a worse time for Londonderry, who was up to his neck in debt after borrowing heavily to build his new harbour. He needed to sell all the coal he could produce to avoid the London banks taking control of his mines and the new harbour.

On the owners' side Londonderry proved to be the weak link in the chain, and he agreed to settle on new terms, conceding a reduction in the hours of labour for boys from 18 to 1 2 hours and better

Thomas Hepburn

hewing prices for the men. Lambton was soon to follow Londonderry's example and by May the owners had been routed.

The new union's victory was however short-lived. On the April binding in 1832 Londonderry, now free from the danger of bankruptcy, renewed his alliance with the owners and they collectively refused to bind any man who was a member of the union. A bloody conflict ensued. The inevitable forced evictions led to armed clashes

between miners and the military. In an effort to break the men's spirit the authorities tried and hanged a Jarrow miner called William Joblin for murder and gibbeted his body at Jarrow Slake.

Hunger, blacklegs and the outbreak of cholera in the villages all conspired to break the union. The men drifted back to work and Hepburn was victimised. In the terminology of the times he became a 'sacrificed man'. Despite this crushing defeat Hepburn tried to revive the Union in 1835, but to no avail.

Hepburn's union had been smashed but the spirit of trade unionism survived. However organisation became looser and localised at pit level. The requirement for miners to sign the bond in the April of each year inevitably created the need for collective action. The union slowly re-grouped at local pits, and Thornley was to become a centre of union activity.

Thornley colliery

Despite the cyclical downturns in trade, demand for coal was increasing and new collieries were being sunk through the limestone to the south.

On January 28 1834 the first sod was cut at the village of Thornley, a small agricultural village boasting a population of 50. The prime mover in this venture was John Gully, a former prize-fighter and once British champion. Even if Gully was perhaps the most colourful of the adventurers who were attracted to East Durham, he was not untypical.

Gully had started life as the lowly son of a butcher and followed his father into that trade. He climbed his way out of poverty by way of the bare-knuckle business. Having spent some time in debtors' prison he became a publican, a professional gambler, a racehorse owner and the betting manager of the Price of Wales. He then tried his hand at politics and had been elected Member of Parliament for Pontefract just before the sinking of Thornley colliery.

Gully was one of the partners involved in the sinking of Hetton Pit and had made a small fortune by selling his share. He had married into an aristocratic family, and Sir William Chater of Witton Castle was his brother-in-law. Chater and Gully formed a partnership known as Gully and Partners, Gully providing the majority of the capital.

The Thornley sinking was typical of its time. The sinkers were Cornishmen who were directed by a number of German technicians. The houses were built of local quarries' limestone, thrown up by a local builder without regard for either the comfort or the health of the future occupants. Thomas Dunlop was paid £20 per house. When this princely sum is compared with the average hewer's wage of £1. per week, or a total sinking investment of £60,000, it is clear that Gully's investment in housing was not extravagant.

Sanitation in the new village consisted of an ash and dung heap at the back of the houses extending the full length of the pit rows. The dirt-floored houses boasted a single room no bigger than four yards by five and a small pantry. Water was drawn from a well at Gore Hall, transported to the village on carts and sold to the miners' families at a penny a bucket.

Green labour

The new pit attracted men from all over Britain, many of them 'green labour' — poor agricultural labourers with no knowledge of pit work. Experienced labour was at a premium and throughout the coalfield there were pitmen of a certain kind requiring jobs. These were the 'sacrificed men' of the 1831-32 disputes. It is difficult to quantify how many of these men made their way to Thornley, since 'marked men' often changed their names when moving from village to village. However, the subsequent history of Thornley has given rise to speculation that more than a few of these old union warriors found their way to approach Gully and Partners for work.

Irish Catholic and Protestant immigrants, green labour from southern counties and old Durham families with their tradition of solidarity and unionism created an explosive social mixture. In 1837 Gully and partners provided the detonator when they appointed Richard Heckles to be the resident viewer of the colliery. Richard Heckles was a mining engineer of distinction and a militant opponent of organised labour.

The miners of Northumberland and Durham were now recovering from the crushing defeat of 1832 and many miners became influenced by the great Chartist movement. No village was more influenced than Thornley.

After the Peterloo massacre in 1819 a huge wave of rebellion swept through the country. This radical movement had entered the lives of the pitmen in the North East of England, who had actively supported the cause of reform. Radical classes had been organised amongst Durham pitmen and Winlaten, on the south bank of the Tyne near Gateshead, was a recognised centre of subversion. The village of Winlaten was known to be armed with rifles and cannon, and the local foundry produced pikes and 'caltrops' spiked instruments placed on the ground to unseat the cavalry. The movement ran out of steam in 1820 after the Cato Street

Conspiracy, when a Government spy averted an attempt to murder the Cabinet of George 111 and declare a provisional Government.

In 1832 the Great Reform Bill was passed through Parliament. It was supposed to give more rights to the ordinary people. While the Act extended the right to vote to some of the middle classes it did nothing to extend democracy to working people. Far from placating reformers the 1832 Act gave rise to the Chartist movement and its call for manhood suffrage, secret ballots, payment for MPs, the abolition of the property qualification for MPs, equal electoral districts and Annual Parliaments.

The Chartist movement began as an alliance between middle-class and working-class forces but as the struggle developed a distinct division between these socially incompatible wings developed.

Middle-class radicals sought to modify the existing system, making it more democratic, but not to destroy it entirely. By 1839 the working-class wing was calling for an end to the government of the rich and for a radical redistribution of wealth. Parliamentary reform was, for this wing of the Chartist movement, just one stage in achieving a more fundamental aim. These more extreme Chartists were to be known as the Physical Force Chartists. The more moderate were known as the Moral Force Chartists. They achieved an unstable unity in the slogan 'peaceably if we can, by force if we must.'

The Durham County Charter Association was formed in Sunderland in November 1838, and turned its attention to agitation in the colliery villages. In March 1839 at their quarterly meeting delegates were in attendance from ten colliery villages. The miners of Thornley were in the forefront of this movement and before long in the colliery workshops at Thornley pit the blacksmiths were busy making pikes and caltrops which they sold to fellow Chartists in other villages.

Chartist Women

The movement was by no means exclusively male. Female Political Unions were founded in the coalfield and in May and June 1839 branches were formed in many mining villages, among them Easington Lane, Haswell and Thornley.

The Chartist paper, the Northern Liberator, reported on June 8 1939 that Elizabeth Mallet of Thornley Association addressed a 320-strong women's meeting saying,

> ' ...that her husband had served with the army and was ready to lead or to follow. She too had learned what pistols were made for, and she would say to her husband, in the words of Ruth, "whither thou goest I will go" even if it were into the mouth of a cannon (loud cheers).

And that Mrs G Smith said that from the the earliest dawn of reason her soul and affections were with the cause of freedom.

In 1839 Chartist agitation throughout the country, reached a peak and many concluded that an armed uprising was imminent. Thomas Reaves and John

Watson were the leaders of the Thornley Chartists, and on Good Friday 1839 they led the Thornley men behind their banner to Pittington Hill to hear John Julian Harney, the northern delegate to the Chartists' 'Parliament' known as the Northern Convention.

In July a leading Chartist, Dr. Taylor was arrested in Birmingham, and a protest meeting was called in Newcastle, after which Harney was arrested and taken into custody. When the news reached Thornley the village erupted in indignation and the pit-head was soon surrounded by angry Chartists who demanded that the banksman call all the men to bank. When the engineman refused to co-operate they took over the engine house and the craftsmen in the workshops downed tools.

On the same night the Thornley Chartists commandeered a locomotive and its wagons on the Durham and Sunderland railway and rode to a Chartists' rally on the Town Moor in Sunderland. That week Thornley colliery remained idle and on Saturday July 13 the village attended a monster rally at Fatfield, where it is said pike heads were openly bought and sold. On their return to Thornley the Chartists besieged a public house where the colliery officials were

drinking. When police who had been drafted into the village arrived to rescue the officials the Riot Act was read by the sergeant in charge. The Chartists replied by turning on the constables, relieving them of their truncheons and beating them without mercy. They escaped more serious harm when Richard Heckles, the colliery viewer, arrived with a band of vigilantes whom he had hastily aroused.

Next day a company of the 98th Regiment of Foot arrived in the village, and under their watchful eyes the pit returned to work.

The excitement of 1839 subsided but the day-to-day problems of the miners remained.

Although miners were forced to sign a yearly bond laying out strict legal conditions regulating the conditions of labour, the degree to which those conditions were enforced varied from pit to pit. The condition of the coal trade also had its effect. If trade was good the owners would tend to be more flexible and overlook little misdemeanours such as miners lying idle on a Monday to recover from the excesses of the weekend, or miners sending short weight or dirty coals to bank. Some owners realised that if they 'played the game' and made sure the weighing machine was accurate and that it carried the government stamp they were likely to encounter less discontent and therefore fewer stoppages.

Richard Heckels was not from this school of thought, ruling with an iron fist. The bond was enforced to the last oppressive detail. Tubs were laid out for the smallest piece of splint, stone or brasses. The weighing machine at bank was faulty; it was unstamped and despite many deputations, he stubbornly refused to have it replaced.

A New County Union

In 1842 the Thornley miners' union was instrumental in establishing a union organisation that once again united the counties of Northumberland and Durham. On January 15 1842 an advertisement appeared in the Chartist paper The Northern Star calling for a meeting on the 22nd of the same month, 'to adopt measures for resistance to the coal owners and their viewers'. The advertisement was signed by Thomas Birrell 'by order of the Thornley Colliery Union'.

The chairman of the meeting was a miner from Wingate called Ben Embleton. Embleton was a true pioneer of unionism among pitmen. His involvement stretched back to the illegal Brotherhood, whose influence among the northern pitmen ebbed and flowed for twenty or so years at the turn of the nineteenth century. He had taken part in the strike of 1810, when the owners had tried to change the yearly bindings from October to January, and he served as one of the leaders with Hepburn in 1831 and 1832. Like Hepburn he was a Primitive Methodist, lay preacher and Chartist.

This Chester-le-Street meeting was not well attended but it did elect Thomas Hall of Thornley to convene a further meeting the next month at Monkwearmouth. The new Northumberland and Durham Miners Association soon became well established and united with the county unions throughout Britain and Ireland in the first national union of mineworkers, which was called The Miners Association of Great Britain and Ireland. Its first meeting was held on November 7 1842 in Wakefield, West Yorkshire.

The Miners Association of Northumberland and Durham engaged a young lawyer by the name of W.P Roberts.

William Prowting Roberts was one of the outstanding men of the 19 th century, and became known as the Miners' Attorney-General. He was born in 1806 the son of a vicar of Chelmsford in Essex. He was educated at Charterhouse public school, and then trained as a solicitor. He first practised in Bath and his first political instinct was to support the Tories. Many have speculated as to what brought about his conversion to the

WP Roberts

cause of working-class politics, but the most likely explanation is his revulsion at the treatment of agricultural labourers. Wiltshire, where he lived, had been at the centre of the Captain Swing riots of 1830 -31.

The introduction of threshing machines had led to seasonal unemployment among farm workers, and they had demanded that the farmers stop using these new machines. When their demands fell on deaf ears they resorted to force and burned down hayricks and barns. Law and order was enforced with an iron fist and 19 labourers were executed, 50 transported and 644 imprisoned. Historians speculate that it was this treatment of half-starving men driven to desperate acts to provide food for their families that offended Roberts' deeply held religious beliefs. Unlike others of his class, Roberts did not become a member of the more liberal wing of the Chartist movement but evolved as a diehard Physical Force Chartist.

In his eventful life he had his life threatened by Wiltshire Tories, survived an assassination attempt and was given a two-year prison sentence for making inflammatory speeches. His defence of the pitmen of Thornley has become a legend.

Matters came to a head in Thornley on November 24 1843, when with the support of the new union the pitmen struck work. Heckles responded by fining all the men a half-crown each and instructing them to make up for the lost day by working the next pay Saturday. The men continued the strike and Heckles responded by invoking the Master and Servant Act. Warrants were duly issued for the arrest of 68 men, all of whom were active in the union. A special court was convened by Durham magistrates to hear the case against the men. Gully and his partners were represented by JE Marshall, and WP Roberts appeared for the men.

The owners' case was simple — yes, the terms of the bond were harsh but it was an agreement that had been freely entered into by the pitmen, and by refusing to work they were in breach of the agreement and should therefore face the penalty of imprisonment.

The situation was inflamed by the conduct of Heckles, who, under cross-examination, agreed that a man could be fined as much as 22 shillings in just one week and then with a grin on his face admitted that men had been fined as much as five and eight shillings regularly. The grin incensed Roberts, and the chairman of the bench intervened with the statement that he could not believe that a man would allow himself to be fined to such a degree.

Roberts trump card was that the weighing machine was unstamped and that this had been admitted by Heckles. Roberts argued that since weighing machines were legally required under the terms of the bond to be stamped the bond was invalid and the fines were therefore illegal. Roberts asked for the trial to be stopped but was overruled by the chairman of the bench.

Roberts then called the miners individually to testify.

First in the dock was John Cookson:

'A man cannot get a living if the bond is carried out in its strictness. If a man is fined for a quart of splint he cannot earn a living. I would rather go to jail than work under such a bond.'

Matthew Dawson:

'It is not so easy now to earn a living as it was three months ago, as the bond was never put into full force till now. I recollect 22 shillings being laid out for one man.'

Thomas Dormant Moran:

'I cannot earn a living if the bond is carried out. I was fined 27 shillings the past fortnight I was paid. I will go to jail rather than work under such a bond.'

John James Bird:

' The steel yards have been a complaint for the past ten months. This was the real cause of the strike, not the 2s 6p fine.'

William Wearmouth:

' The bond has never been enforced before for a quart of stones. Now an honest man cannot get a living. I would rather stop in jail for ever than work under this bond'.

George Nesbitt:

' It is impossible to send up a tub without a quart of stones. It is the feeling of the men generally that they would rather go to prison than work for nothing'.

By this time the Chairman was getting a little irritated by the repetitive nature of the evidence and he asked Roberts if he had any different evidence to put before the bench. Roberts replied that there were between 300 and 400 hewers involved and it was his intention to bring every one before the court to testify as to his intentions. Clearly daunted by this ordeal the magistrates opted to adjourn the case until the next day to see if some compromise could be reached between the masters and the men.

When the court reconvened the following day the chairman asked if any agreement had been reached. Roberts replied, 'none', and called his first witness William Henderson, who made the now standard statement that he would rather go to prison than work under the terms of the bond.

A resounding cry went round the court,

 'W'll all gan! W'll all gan!'

The trial dragged on all through the day as pitman after pitman testified to the impossible conditions of the bond. Finally it was time for Roberts to sum up his case for the defence.

He asked that the magistrates show mercy since under the Master and Servant Act the men were not allowed to be tried by jury. He was not pleading for mercy in the normal sense, since he did not consider that the men he represented were guilty of any crime. On the contrary Roberts argued the men who should really be in the dock were the masters and Heckles. The Act, he said,

gave the magistrates the power to send the men to prison — 'must it always be imprisonment as if the men were always criminals and the masters were all angels?.

Marshall, for the owners, was clinical: the men had bound themselves under the terms of the bond for a period of twelve months. The bond required that the men do not absent themselves from work. They had broken the terms of the bond and were therefore guilty.

Of course they were found guilty and immediately removed to the house of correction in Durham to serve a sentence of six weeks.

Roberts had one further trick up his sleeve. He immediately set off for London and returned with a writ of habeas corpus. On his presenting the writ, the prisoners were removed to the Court of the Queens Bench and acquitted.

When Roberts returned to Thornley two days later he was met on the outskirts of the village by a crowd of miners and their families who removed the horses from the shafts of the carriage and pulled the coach through the village in celebration.

The Thornley victory boosted the confidence of the county's pitmen and increased the pressure on the leaders of the new union to rectify the harsh conditions forced upon them by the bond. On

March 2, 20,000 pitmen met on Shadons Hill and agreed that they would not bind themselves until after the National Conference to be held in Glasgow on March 25 1844.

The Glasgow Conference was attended by representatives of 70,000 miners. Durham and Northumberland pressed the conference to call a national strike but were narrowly defeated.

Ben Embleton, from Wingate, one of the Durham delegates, appealed to the conference saying that he knew as much of the miners of Northumberland and Durham as any man and he fully believed that if they allowed them to fight their own battle and keep their men [i.e., miners from the other coalfields] from filling their places, they would come off victorious.

Martin Jude, the treasurer of the Northumberland and Durham miners, was more cautious and counselled against taking action alone. Embleton, however, won the day and permission was granted for Durham and Northumberland to proceed alone with the assistance of the National Miners Association.

Murton colliery was at this time known as the Dalton Winning, and after a long and ruinous battle against the sand feeder had just reached the coal. The owners were facing bankruptcy and were understandably anxious to produce as much coal as possible. When on April 5 the miners of the two counties terminated their bond and refused to be bound on the owners' terms, the owners were keen to bribe the Dalton men into blacklegging.

After the strike was declared, 35,000 to 40,000 miners assembled at Shadons HIll. When John Tulip, prior to moving a resolution, informed the meeting that the Dalton men were present on the field, according to Fynes in his *History of the Northumberland and Durham Miners*:

> 'The whole mass of the miners rose to their feet and gave long and tremendous cheering.'

The owners struck back with their usual tactics. Throughout the two counties families were evicted from their cottages, and the military was brought in to occupy the villages, intimidate the miners and protect the 'Candy men'. Candy men were the riff-raff of Newcastle and Sunderland whom the owners traditionally hired to turn the miners out of their houses. Despite all the efforts of the new union, some miners were recruited to

Martin Jude

replace the strikers. At Seaton Delaval in Northumberland Welshmen were persuaded to take the place of the miners and occupy their cottages.

Londonderry had a ready supply of labour on his Irish estates which he introduced into his collieries in an attempt to re-start production.

Miners, many of them now living in camps on the lanes, sold what they had to provide food which was shared out among the community. Shop-owners gave credit, much to the annoyance of Londonderry, who issued the following proclamation to the shopkeepers and traders of Seaham:

'Lord Londonderry again warns all the shopkeepers and tradesmen in his town of Seaham that if they still give credit to pitmen who hold off work and continue in the union, such men will be marked by his agents and overmen, and will never be employed in his colliery again, and the shopkeepers may be assured that they will never have any custom or dealings with them from Lord Londonderry's large concerns that he can in any manner prevent.

'Lord Londonderry further informs the traders and shopkeepers that having by his measures increased very largely the last year's trade to Seaham, and if this credit is so improperly and fatally given to his unreasonable pitmen, thereby prolonging the injurious strike, it is his firm determination to carry back all the outlay of his concerns even to Newcastle.

'Because it is neither fair, just or equitable that the resident traders in his own town should combine and assist the infatuated workmen and pitmen in prolonging their own miseries by continuing an insane strike, and an unjust senseless warfare against their proprietors and masters'.

At this time their were no pits in Seaham, the closest being the Dalton Winning at Murton, but many pitmen must have been in the habit of shopping in that area.

Third Marquis of Londonderry

The men and their families held out for 18 weeks, until hunger and despair forced them back to work on the owners' terms. By August nearly all the pits in Durham had returned. The Northumberland men held on longer but after unsuccessful attempts to restart the strike in Durham they too were forced to return.

Many of the leaders were sacrificed, among them the old campaigner Ben Embleton, who spent the next years touring the pit villages holding meetings and keeping the spirit of trade unionism alive. He was known for his habit of banging a blazer outside the pit rows to attract a crowd. He was immortalised in the folk song written by George Purdon of South Pelaw:

Bang the bleazer Ben, bang the bleazer Ben,
Cry: Fear ye not the masters, join the union men!
The year was 1844, the big strike had been lost.
Trudged the miners back to work to reckon up the cost
Of twenty weeks privation, not one concession won.
The men they were ten times worse off than when the strike began

Bang the bleazer Ben, bang the bleazer Ben,
Cry: Fear ye not the masters, join the union men!

The union tried to rally but meetings were few.
There was no work for union men if e'er the masters knew.
To stir the old emotions on the Wear and Tyne,
The brave old Ben Embleton kept banging out his rhyme.

By 1847 Embleton was driven to a state of abject poverty. Now an old man, who had served the cause of unionism for over 37 years, he appealed through the pages of the Miners' Advocate, the paper of the National Miners Association, for help:

'Brethren I appeal to you. Shall I, who have fought so long in the good cause, be visited by starvation? Shall I be obliged to seek the shelter of an infamous Poor Law Bastille, wherein to lay down my body to die. Shall I be driven to the hard necessity of ending my life on parish pay? For the sake of union principles.'

We can only imagine the depths of despair that drove this proud man to make such an appeal.

Chapter 2

High Pit Seaham, London Illustrated News

The Hetton Coal Company began the sinking of the first pit in the Seaham area at Seaton in 1845 to a depth of 1819 ft. This first shaft was called Seaton colliery but was later to be known as the High pit.

On April 13 1849 Londonderry began the sinking of Seaham colliery, just 150 yards east from Seaton Colliery. The new shaft, which was to become known as the Low Pit, finally reached a depth of 1797 ft and it drew its first coal on March 27 1852.

From its infancy this pit was to be a source of misery and controversy, and the scars for many have not yet faded. By the June of 1852 no fewer than three explosions had occurred at the High Pit, the third leading to the loss of six lives. John Defty 53, Charles Halliday 10, John Pratt 20, John Simpson 27, and Andrew Simpson 18, all perished. This was one of the first explosions to be investigated by a Mines Inspector. Legislation establishing the Mines Inspectorate had been passed in 1850, a measure opposed by Londonderry, who had declared that no inspector would be allowed in his mines and if any inspector did enter his mines then he might stay there. The government took Londonderry's statement seriously enough to insert a clause in the Bill establishing that an inspector had the right to enter a mine *but also to gain egress from that mine.*

Inquest

The inquest on the six dead men was first adjourned to allow the Inspector of Mines to be present. It re-opened on Wednesday June 23 at the Mill Inn, after which an historic meeting was to take place on the same premises. The eminent mining engineers, among them TE Foster, Matthias Dunn, TC Naynard and GB Forster, discussed the establishment of the Northern Institute of Mining and Mechanical Engineers. For the first time mining was achieving the status of a science and the notion was slowly dawning that scientific knowledge may perhaps prevent disasters.

The Third Marquis of Londonderry was not to see the fruits of this new age of enlightenment. By 1854 he had died. He had lived long enough to build a new rail link from Seaham to the docks at Sunderland. Seaham Harbour was now working to capacity and could not handle the coal from the new winning.

On the January 16 1862 at Hartley Colliey, Northumberland the massive beam of the pumping engine fractured and plummeted down the shaft, with devastating consequences. The beam tore down all the shaft furnishings before it jammed in the shaft above the highest level. This one-shaft colliery was then sealed by the falling debris, trapping 204 men and boys underground. As the lethal fumes from the underground ventilation furnace slowly invaded the workings the entombed pitmen slowly suffocated. Not one survived.

This tragedy horrified the nation and prompted a hitherto unwilling Government to introduce legislation requiring all new collieries to have a second means of egress provided by a second shaft or drift, and by January 1 1865, all collieries were to have a second means of egress.

In 1862 neither Seaton or Seaham collieries were required by this Act to have two shafts. However, the sheer horror of the Hartley disaster, and perhaps pressure from the miners, brought about a rare collaboration between competing coal companies, and a roadway was constructed between the workings of the two collieries. Not one moment too soon. On March 29 1862 the cage rope at Seaham colliery snapped, sending the cage careering down the shaft, demolishing the timber brattice that divided the shaft into its upcast and downcast components. The cage jammed in the shaft, and dislodged stone falling on to the cage blocked the shaft. 300 to 400 men and boys were at work below and would no doubt have shared the fate of the Hartley victims had there not been an escape through the workings of Seaton colliery.

As the 1865 deadline, requiring all collieries to have two shafts, approached, Londonderry's widow Lady Francis bought Seaton Colliery from the Hetton Coal Company, amalgamating them into one colliery. Seaton shaft now became known as the High pit and the Seaham shaft the Low pit.

While Scaham Colliery was the official name of the combined colliery everyone referred to it as the 'Nicky-Nack' or the 'Nack,' a name it retained until its closure in 1986.

Folklore offers two explanations for this strange nickname. A popular belief is that the winding engines of the colliery made a distinctive nicky-nack sound. However, the famous Seaham historian John E McCutcheon, in his book

Low pit, Seaham, London Illustrated News

Troubled Seams, offers another explanation.

The local windmill owner Tommy Chilton, who was also the landlord of the Mill Inn, became known as Tommy 'Nicky Nack' Chilton, for his deftness in 'fettling' spinning wheels whose knack-reels made a nicky-nack sound at regular intervals. The name was transferred to the Mill Inn and then to the colliery.

Whatever the truth of these theories there was no mistaking the origins of its other nickname, 'The Hell Pit'. The tendency for one part of the mine to produce large quantities of methane gas had tragic results.

The latter half of the 1860s became a landmark in the history of Durham miners. Since the defeat of the 1844 strike the pitmen of the county of Durham had been without a county union but not entirely without any union at all. In 1860, in order to eliminate the numerous disputes involving miners who were fined for short weight, an Act of Parliament was passed giving miners the right to elect and pay one of their number to check the weight of the coal drawn to bank. This led to the establishment of pit-based unions organised around the election of checkweighmen.

The checkweighman often became the secretary of these lodges and conducted negotiations with the owners when this was required. In Durham these checkweighmen were often Primitive Methodists, chosen by the men for their honesty, sobriety and strong union principles.

In 1869 a strike at Wearmouth colliery in which WP Roberts again played an important role stimulated a campaign to establish a county union. The pits of South East Durham proved the most fertile ground. One of the principal meetings in this campaign was held at Thornley on Saturday September 25 1869 and addressed by Messrs. Burt and Wood and organised by J Collage of Murton and C Nicholson of Seaham.

New Union Established

By 1870 the union was starting to get established as a force on the coalfield, the largest branches being Murton with 342 members, Thornley with 230, Trimdon with 165 and Seaham with 150.

One of the first actions of the new union was to represent the interests of the miners at Wheatley Hill colliery, where five men had lost their lives due to an inundation of water. Owners had long been insulated, by their viewers, from any blame for these tragedies. Although more legislation governing mining practice was in existence actual prosecutions were rare. In matters legal their was an amazing degree of solidarity between mine-owners and the judiciary.

The inquest on the these five men at Wheatley Hill concluded that;

'The deceased were killed on the 19th of January by a burst of water in Wheatley Hill pit through the gross negligence of W Spencer, head viewer, W Hay, resident viewer, and Thomas Watson, overman; and that the said W.Spence, W Hay and T Watson did kill and slay the five deceased previously mentioned by neglecting to put in proper bore holes for the safe working of the mine.'

The accused were then committed to trial at the Assizes on a charge of manslaughter.

These men were committed to trial because they had violated a clause in the 1860 Mines Act requiring the owners to ensure that bore holes were drilled in advance of a drivage where it was suspected quantities of water had collected.

For pitmen so long denied justice this must have seemed a revolutionary verdict. But it was not to

Puffing Billy, Wheatley Hill colliery 1864

be, and justice was to elude the new union. The trial judge, no doubt conscious of a dangerous precedent that may have been set, ruled that the pitman Roberts, in whose flat the water broke, should have known of the danger as well as the manager. The men's counsel withdrew and the viewers were acquitted.

Despite this setback the union was steadily gaining ground and influence. The first delegate meeting was held on March 25 1871 and the following resolutions were passed:

1. That coal hewed by pit men be measured by weight and not by volume.

2. That checkweighmen be the choice of the pitmen whether or not they were bound men at the colliery.

3. That mines be inspected by the Mines Inspector at intervals of not less than 3 months

4. That no boys to be allowed to work more than 10 hrs a day. (Submitted by Murton Lodge)

The second resolution regarding checkweighmen was no doubt a result of the situation at Thornley colliery, where the colliery manager had refused to bind A Cairns, the men's checkweighman. The condition that the checkweighman had to be bound effectively gave the owners a veto over who should be elected.

The new County Union was not without its internal problems, which emanated from the peculiar way in which unions had developed in Durham as pit-based unions with strong ties with the local community. The union was an integral part of the community, and at a time when most working men were disfranchised the union was their local government.

Durham miners had a reputation for firing from the hip. When disputes arose they were quick to take action without the sanction of their area leaders.

Seaham Dispute

On May 17 1872 a dispute developed at Seaham colliery over the length of hours worked and the shift times of hewers and putters. The Seaham lodge struck work without the sanction of the Area Committee, provoking an angry response from William Crawford, the Area Secretary. He wasted no time in telling the Seaham men of his feelings and dispatched to them a short and succinct telegram:

' Do go to work. You must know you are wrong. You will get no support. Liable to punishment.'

The Seaham men were incensed and at subsequent meetings Crawford was the subject of some verbal abuse. He remained unrepentant, telling the men, in as many words, that just because they paid his wages he was not obliged to agree with them.

The dispute causing this clash of opinions had been festering since the previous year

On Tuesday October 24 1871 the putter boys at Seaham colliery held a mass meeting to protest about the conditions of the bond which determined their hours of labour. They were compelled to rise every morning at 3.00 am and did not ride out of the pit until 6.00 pm at night.

The Viewer Mr Dakes to whom they sent a deputation refused to give them an answer until the bond expired in April.

The putter boys resolved to lay the pit idle but were restrained by other classes of pitmen who wanted to organise a deputation with Drakes on their own behalf before any action was taken. When Dakes refused to see them they convened a further mass meeting on the Thursday of that week.

This meeting never took place. Fate once more intervened at the 'Hell Pit'. At 11.30 pm on Wednesday October 25 Thomas Hutchinson and his son were working at 'The Curve', a curved roadway connecting the two shafts of the colliery. They were preparing to fire a shot in order to blast down a portion of stone to widen the roadway. The shot was fired and an explosion ripped

William Crawford

through the workings, killing 26 men, one of whom was Hutchinson's son.

After igniting the touch paper of the shot the son had run in-bye, the father out-bye. The son had taken up a position in-bye, acting as a sentry to prevent other pitmen accidentally walking into the shot. This arbitrary choice of directions made by the father and son proved a matter of life and death.

At the inquest Hutchinson was unshakeable in his

evidence that the firing of the shot and the explosion had occurred simultaneously. Even under cross examination he asserted:

> ' I am not going too tell a lie for any man on earth; our shot went off just as the explosion came — just as two men may be running and come to collision'.

The management of the colliery were reluctant to accept that the firing of a gunpowder shot had caused the explosion and the jury agreed with them, declaring a verdict of accidental death due to an explosion caused by the release of gas from the roof of No. 2 bankhead of No. 3 pit. The verdict was roundly condemned in the local press. But what concerned the community more was the owners' decision to erect brick stoppings and wall in the bodies of 22 of the victims, a measure they insisted was necessary to save the pit from fire.

By the Saturday of that week the ventilation furnaces had been relit and the colliery resumed coal-work on the Monday. It was not until December 10 that the bodies of the victims were finally recovered and given a proper burial.

Despite the ever present danger of sudden death the 1870s looked full of promise for the Northern pitmen. France and Prussia were at war, and the coalfield of Alsace and Lorraine was their battle field. With this major competitor out of action coal was at a premium and prices were rising.

For the first time in the history of coalmining the owners began to think the unthinkable — should they recognise the new Union and negotiate with them?

On February 17 1872 the executive of the DMA, now representing the overwhelming majority of pitmen, was invited to meet with the owners. The union accepted and over the course of the year negotiated two general advances in wages and, more important, abolished that relic of feudal serfdom, the yearly bond.

Social commentators in the nineteenth century commented, usually in disapproving terms, on the role of women on the Great Northern Coalfield — they were often seen drinking with their men folk in the beer shops, expressing forthright opinions and when riot ensued they were often in the front line.

Just as the Chartist agitation of 1839 was not exclusively male-dominated, so the new confidence and fighting spirit of the 1870s involved the women of the pit communities.

Butchers' meat, a luxury beyond the reach of most of Britain's poor labourers, was as important to hewers of coal as coal was to a steam engine. Meat was supplied to the pit villages by butchers who traded from the back of horse-drawn vans. In 1872 the butchers increased the price of meat and the women of the villages were outraged. The price of milk, potatoes and vegetables was also affected, which further inflamed the situation. The women believed that the traders were taking advantage of the improved circumstances of the miners. They resolved to fight.

On Wednesday June 12 1872, 300 women from Murton gathered on a field on the outskirts of the village to protest at the price increases. They elected Martin Thompson, the miners' checkweighman, as the chairman of the meeting. This was the only concession made to the menfolk, the rest of the meeting being conducted only by women. They then proceeded to fix the price of meat, milk and potatoes at a level they were prepared to pay and resolved to boycott all traders whose prices exceeded this level.

Following the example of the Murton women, women in the surrounding villages organised meetings, deliberately excluding men with the exception of one or two who were asked to perform certain organisational functions, such as reporting the meetings to the press.

On Thursday June 13 200 women met at Seaham. They identified those women who were not observing the boycott and ' tin-panned ' them, shaming them to conform to the wishes of the majority.

An even larger meeting of 1,000 women assembled in Seaham five days later and miners wives were joined by those women who worked in the bottle works, the iron works and the chemical works. Prior to the meeting the union 'Crake Man', the union equivalent of a town crier,

had been sent round the town announcing the prices that the women had set.

The meeting was at first addressed by Mr Kellet, the miners' union delegate, but when he was heckled by women suggesting that he should have sent his wife instead, he withdrew as chairman of the meeting in favour of Mary Errington, who was reported to have had with her a young child whom she was feeding.

The meeting resolved to form a women's Union and Mary was elected president. She addressed the meeting,

> ' And we'll have to frighten the men that oppose us. I wish I had been a man. (Great cheers and laughter) We are ordered to be quiet, to keep silence in the church....we are not going to be frightened, but you must excuse me if I am going too far. ("No, no" and cries of "go on, you will make all right; if not we will have a bonny lot of men offering to speak"). Petticoat government's been a long time in starting, but we will exert our rights, and prove faithful to our cause.'

The movement spread like a forest fire throughout Durham, as far as Oakenshaw in the West and Jarrow in the North. Meetings were convened and the women raised their standard, a tricolour flag of pink, white and calico.

Butchers who dared enter the villages were terrorised by crowds of women banging anything that would create a din. Their anger was not directed only at the meat traders. Strikebreakers were equally at risk.

The Sunderland Times reported that:

> ' The good ladies of Seaton Colliery on Friday took part in a demonstration against a poor woman. The wife of a brakesman had committed a contravention of the general agreement by purchasing her usual quantity of beef, this led to upwards of 300 women turning up with fire blazers, trays, etc round the woman's residence, and for a lengthened time the greatest disorder prevailed. The miners, colliery officials, shopkeepers, innkeepers, and even the colliery doctor are prohibited from buying butchers' meat at the current prices.

> 'On Saturday the Matrons of Seaham Colliery, taking advantage of the absence of their husbands at the Durham Gala, made another demonstration at the house of the unfortunate woman. They marched to the rendezvous with an effigy of their victim, which was placed at the front of her dwelling, and soon reduced it to ashes amidst the wildest uproar and excitement. Not satisfied with this ebullition the "ladies" vented their indignation upon the railings on the front door, which they pulled up bodily, a volley of stones being directed by way of a finale against the house.'

1880 Explosion

By 1880 Seaham colliery was producing 500,000 tons of coal a year and employing 1,500 men and boys. It was the jewel in the crown of the Londonderry enterprises, making the major contribution to its considerable wealth.

On Wednesday September 8 1880, 231 men and boys were at work underground. 169 were working in the Hutton, Low Main, and Maudlin seams. To the east of the Low Pit shaft a drop fault or dipper throws the seams down in such a way that a roadway driven from the Harvey seam through the fault emerged in the Low main seam and at the farthest extent the Low Main and the Maudlin seam converge.

At the Main coal staple a small group of men were engaged in enlarging refuge holes. The clearance between the sides of the roadways and the tubs on the rolly ways was never more than a few inches. Refuge holes were cut in the sides of the roadways to allow men travelling to escape being crushed by the tubs.

A similar group of men were enlarging refuge holes at the curve, the curved-road way between the two shafts, exactly the same place as the disputed seat of the 1870 explosion. At 2.20 am Brown, one of the men working at the Curve, fired a shot and the pit exploded with such force that it was heard as far away as Murton colliery.

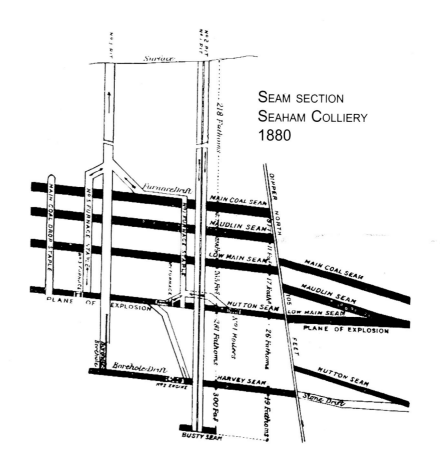

SEAM SECTION
SEAHAM COLLIERY
1880

Of the 231 men working underground 164 perished, some in the the first blast of the explosion but the majority being poisoned when after damp slowly spread through the pit. Many were still alive 24 hours after the first blast and could only wait and hope for rescue. They waited in vain passing the time in prayer. Some wrote messages to their loved ones, etching them on

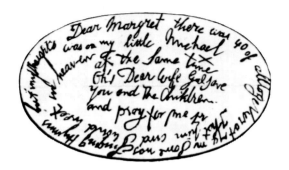

their tin water bottles or in chalk on the sides of tubs or on planks of wood.

Michael Smith, whose young son Michael had died the day before, scratched on his water bottle this last poignant letter to his wife:

'Dear Margaret,

There was 40 of us altogether at 7,00 am. Some were singing hymns, but my thoughts was on my little Michael that him and I would meet in heaven at the same time. O dear god save you and the children, and pray for me.....Dear wife farewell. My last thoughts are about you and the children. Be sure and learn the children to pray for me. O what an awful position we are in.'

As the rescuers fought their way into the Hutton seam above them a line of carts filled with straw waited in the pit yard to transport the dead bodies back home. In the joiners' workshops the joiners set about making coffins. The whole town assembled around the pit heapstead, fathers, mothers and children — still hopeful that, perhaps by some miracle, their loved one had survived.

It soon became apparent that the Maudlin Seam was on fire. Men were still barred in and it was impossible to know for certain if anyone was still alive. Londonderry and his agents decided that saving the Maudlin Coal was more important than the sensibilities of the pitmen and their families and began to erect brick stoppings to wall off the Maudlin Seam before the trapped miners had been reached.

At first the pitmen reluctantly accept the situation, but with the horror of the 1871 explosion still fresh in their minds the burden of grieving for 164 men and boys, some as young as 13, was too much for the community to bear. The belief persisted that the men trapped in the Maudlin seam were still alive when the stoppings had been erected.

Coal-work restarted in November but the strain of working whilst the bodies of their comrades remained entombed in the Maudin seam erupted into anger, and by

Rescuers at work

the second week of December the colliery was laid idle. The men refused to work any longer until the stoppings were taken down and the bodies removed.

Londonderry was unmoved, and the strike continued through December and January. By February of 1881 Londonderry was importing blacklegs into the colliery to take the place of the Seaham men. Riots and intimidation ensued and men were arrested and jailed. As usual the men arrested were often union leaders who denied being present when the disturbances had taken place.

The Durham Chronicle commented:

'The Coal Owners Association threatened the men with all the terror which a summons from a Police Court and an eviction from their homes could possess, in order to compel them to resume work.'

Sacrificed Men

The men struggled on until March, when although the majority of the men voted to continue the strike they failed to achieve the two-thirds majority require by the rules of the DMA. Londonderry refused to re-employ all the men. At first 29 men were to be 'sacrificed' but this was finally reduced to eight; Thomas Banks, John Bell, Thomas Brown, Thomas Burt, David Corkhill, John Furness, Robert Newham, and Ralph Pallister. The eight men were ordered to quit their colliery houses. Banks, Brown, Burt and Newham refused and were evicted by force.

The inquest into the deaths of the 164 victims began six days after the fatal explosion. The coroner was anxious to hear the evidence from the witnesses while it was still fresh in their minds.

Establishing the cause of the explosion was vital to the future safety, not just of Seaham colliery but coal mining in general. For some time miners had suspected that coal dust played an important role in pit explosions and this theory proved to be a central feature of the inquest.

As long as there had been coal mines it had been recognised that fire damp (methane gas) and air created an explosive mixture.

The Sunderland Society had been established as early as 1815 to devise a safe lamp to be used in coal mines. Both Sir Humphry Davy, George Stephenson and Dr. Clanny had invented lamps. These lamps all worked on the principle that a wire gauze surrounding the naked flame diffused the heat of the flame, preventing it igniting the gas outside the lamp. The real value of the new lamps was that they could detect the presence of gas. If methane gas was present in the atmosphere the flame in the safety lamp would assume a triangular yellow cap, indicating that methane was burning inside the lamp. In this situation the

Richard Fynes

sensible course of action was to extinguish all lamps since the lamps were not safe where the gas was present in certain concentrations and in strong currents of air.

Paradoxically the introduction of the safety lamp led to a greater loss of life, as men were sent to work in gassy parts of the mine previously impossible to work with a candle.

Richard Fynes commented in 1873:

'The Davy lamp having been introduced, the well known Mr Buddle [Viewer to Londonderry and others] gave it as his opinion that it was a safe lamp for the miners to work with in fiery collieries and all collieries adopted it as such. Experience, however, proved that they were the most deadly instrument ever devised in mining operations and were the cause of more sacrifice of human life than ever occurred before. The fact was that men having confidence in the lamp, the use of which was a guarantee of safety, did not take the same precautions as they would have done had they not had any lamp at all and the reliance on the efficiency of the invention can be traced as the cause of many of the accidents that occurred'.

It was improved ventilation with the introduction of ventilation furnaces at the bottom of the up cast shafts that had made the greatest contribution to pit safety. The strong air current generated as the hot gases from the furnace rose throughout the shaft drew air and any methane gas out of the workings of the pit.

Even with the new methods of ventilation, however, explosions persisted and often pits exploded with a force that was hard to explain when the concentration of methane was so low. Pitmen and some eminent scientist began to form the view that a small quantity of methane in a pit could act as a detonator to a coal dust explosion. Coal dust suspended in the atmosphere, they suspected, created the same explosive mix as methane. It only took a small explosion to create a cloud of coal dust which when driven by the initial explosion through the workings gave rise to a chain reaction, each explosion leading to another.

At the Seaham enquiry a further question was posed: if it was unlikely that even a small amount of methane was present so close to the shaft as the Curve, was it possible that firing a gunpowder shot could itself have detonated a dust cloud explosion?

Coal dust shaken from the continuous passage of full tubs through this part of the mine lay thick on the floor. The theory was advanced that the two stone men kicked up a cloud of coal dust as they ran away from the shot and that this cloud dust was ignited by the shot itself.

Firing a gunpowder shot was a perilous and arduous business. A hole had first to be drilled in the stone. Although the first compressed-air power tools were in use in some mines most drilling was done by sheer muscle power. An iron rod with a hardened chisel tip would be driven into the stone with a large mell-hammer or by twisting a drill rod with a crank handle.

The hole was then charged with powder and entrance to the hole stemmed with clay. A straw filled with powder known as a 'kitty' was then pushed through the clay to make contact with the powder inside. The shot firer would then put a wire through the gauze of his safety lamp and heat it over the flame until it glowed red. After igniting the kitty with the red hot wire the shotfirer ran as fast as he could to a place of safety.

If the shot was contained by the clay the force of the explosion would be towards the stone, which became dislodged. If, as was often the case, the shot blew out then the explosion took place in the roadway.

Owners opposition

The owners were reluctant to accept the coal dust theory. Perhaps they were looking to the cost of controlling dust in a coal mine and the implications of cutting through stone without the aid of gunpowder. Miners and their supporters in Parliament, however, had been conscious of the dangers of using gunpowder for some time.

In 1847, after a great deal of agitation in the coalfields, an amendment to the Mines Act was introduced into parliament, seeking to ban the use of candles and gunpowder in mines. This Bill failed to pass into legislation due to lack of support. One MP who asked for it to be withdrawn was the member from South Durham, Lord Harry Vane, son of the Third Marquis of Londonderry, soon to become in 1853 the Fourth Marquis.

In determining the cause of the 1880 explosion

the jury was called upon to consider two theories, one put forward by Londonderry's viewers, the other by the miners' union and the Government Inspector.

Conflicting Theories

Londonderry's agents put forward the theory that a fall had occurred prior to the explosion in the No 1 Hutton district at the Polka way end, which had resulted in a escape of gas from the strata, and that this gas had been ignited by the safety lamp of a miner called Ramshaw and spread throughout the pit. If this theory was accepted then the explosion was an 'act of god' and the verdict could only be accidental death.

The second theory, supported by the DMA representing the men and the Mines Inspectors was that when the stone man Brown had fired his shot the gunpowder explosion had created a coal dust explosion which had radiated from the Curve. If this theory was accepted then the explosion was due to the practice of shot firing and the owners were at fault.

The evidence for the second of these theories was compelling and was as follows:

1. The 1871 explosion had happened at the exact moment that a shot had been fired at exactly the same point in the pit. This was too rare an occurrence as to be deemed a coincidence.

2. The fact that the area around Brown's shot was undisturbed for several yards in both directions was consistent with the pattern of destruction caused by an explosion in a confined space. Those who favoured the first theory could not explain how a shock wave from in-bye could emanate out-bye and leave a section undisturbed and then continue its destruction once having passed the area of Brown's shot.

In the official report, RS Wright, of the Home Office, referred to this point:

'For about 80 yards in the immediate neighbourhood of Brown's shot (B on the sketch) and thence to the curve there was little, if any, perceptible damage or disturbance. Timbers were not displaced, tools leaning against the wall were not even thrown down. This is consistent with a view that the the explosion commenced at or near Brown's shot and thence radiated into all the three intakes, because colliery explosions often exert but little force at the point of their origin. It is hardly consistent with the view of the proprietors. **Even the caprice of an explosion can hardly explain how a section of 80 yds could escape injury in the main pathway of a blast which (on the proprietors' view) had ruined a mile of gallery on one side of this section , and after passing it ruined to an even a greater degree more than half a mile of galleries on the other side of it.** No solution of this objection to the proprietors' view has been suggested'.

3. The union pointed out that the timber from the area of the fall which the owners insisted

was the seat of the explosion was not crushed and twisted under the weight of the roof, which would have been the case if the fall had accrued due to the pressure of the roof. The timber was straight, consistent with it having been blown out by an explosion occurring at some other point in the mine. The representatives of the owners were unable to refute this fact.

In the official report, RS Wright makes a damming comment on the owners' theory that a fall led to an escape of gas:

'The great objection to this suggestion is that it is **pure assumption based on no evidence whatever**....[emphasis added]. Further according to the evidence of Mr. Foreman, on behalf of the miners, which no witness was called to contradict, and on which he was not cross-examined, the timbers which supported the roof of the site of the fall were not broken or crushed, and were actually blown out of their places southward, not from, but towards the lamp at which according to the proprietors' view the gas must have exploded. If this is correct, it appears to show nearly conclusively that the fall followed instead of preceding the explosion; and the only suggestion by which gas was attempted to be accounted for being negative, the explosion would be entirely inexplicable'.[sic]

4. A chemist, Professor Able, simulated a coal dust explosion using the dust from that part of the mine. While he could not confirm that a shot could ignite a coal dust cloud he could prove that a very small concentration of methane gas, less than could be detected, could act as a detonator to a coal dust explosion.

Summing Up

In his summing up the coroner put the following questions to the jury

1. Does the evidence satisfy you that the explosion occurred at the Polka way end, from either a sudden outburst of gas or from any other cause?

2. If you say no to the first question, does it satisfy you that it occurred in shot firing in the stone drift alluded to?

3. If you say no to the first question and yes to the second or you are not satisfied either way, than I go on to the third question - is shot firing in stone, as at present carried out, in your opinion safe, or does it require further safeguards or restrictions?

4. Then fourth, after professor Ables comprehensive report on coal-dust and its probable connection with explosions, is it in your opinion necessary for the safety of men either to water it or to remove it?

If you will consider these questions and answer them then I think you will have your verdict.

The jury retired at 1.45 pm on April 13 1881 and returned into court an hour later with their verdict.

Verdict of the Jury

The Foreman of the jury gave their verdict:

' We have come to the conclusion that we all agree that an explosion took place, causing the deaths of James Brown and others, at Seaham colliery on the 8th of September 1881; but as to the seat of the explosion we have not been able to determine. As to the other question of firing shots and clearing away coal dust we think that that may safely be left in the hands of the managers.'

For a jury to fly in the face of the facts in such a blatant and obvious manner was not unusual in a town where the coal company was all powerful.

One year after the jury gave their verdict on the Seaham Explosion, on February 16 1882 Trimdon Grange colliery exploded with the loss of 69 lives. Once again the union pointed the finger at the owners and the practice of firing shots, this time in coal. On this occasion the evidence that a gunpowder shot was responsible was less clear and the verdict that the explosion had been caused by a fall of stone releasing gas from the goaf was more convincing.

On December 2, 1886 Elemore pit, owned by the Hetton Coal Company exploded killing 28 men. The circumstances were almost identical to the Seaham explosion of 1880. A shot had been fired in the shaft area, simultaneously the pit had fired and the evidence pointed to that shot creating a coal dust explosion. On this occasion the jury took two hours to decide that there was insufficient evidence to show what had caused the explosion.

Again the coroner invited the jury to make a statement as to the safety of shotfiring.

The coroner asked:

'Do you make any presentment on the subject of shotfiring?'

A juror: 'No, not at all'

Although once again the jury got the coal company off the hook, the tide was finally turning against the use of shot firing and from the date of this accident the practice of using gunpowder in the Hetton coal company mines was terminated. In future where blasting was necessary they were to use — 'gelatine dynamite, in water cartridges, the charges being fired by electricity'.

A collier brig in Seaham docks 1904

Chapter 3

Joiners and fitters, New Seaham colliery 1893

A new era was dawning in the development of mining engineering. Electricity and compressed air had now become a practical means of transmitting the power of steam into the mine in a safer and more convenient form. As industry adopted electrical power there was demand for more and more coal to power the generators. By the 1890's the old collieries that had been successfully sunk through the limestone in the mid-nineteenth century at Hetton, Seaham,

Shotton, Wingate and Thornley had all been extensively worked. The enormous capital cost of the initial sinking had forced a rapid and intensive production regime.

The coroner had noted at the Seaham inquest in 1880 the extensive development of Seaham colliery and had raised the question that perhaps it was too extensive to be safely worked from just two shafts.

The coastal strip to the south of Seaham was still virgin land untouched by the ravages of this extractive industry. By the turn of the century this area was to be transformed into the highest concentration of monster collieries in the British coalfields. Just as electricity and compressed air was encroaching on the life of the miners a new and revolutionary technique, that of shaft freezing, was to transform the lives of the sinkers. The last and final expansion of the Durham coalfield was poised to begin.

The first of these new pits was sunk by the Sixth Marquis of Londonderry at Dawdon. The first sod was cut on the site of the first shaft on August 26 1899 by his wife Theresa, who, as tradition determined, gave her name to the shaft. The second shaft was called the Castlereagh, after his son Lord Castlereagh. To avoid the long and debilitating battle with the sand feeder he employed the Poetsch method of freezing the shaft area. Dawdon colliery was the second pit to be sunk in county Durham by this method. The first was the Gelbe colliery at Washington earlier that year. Despite the obvious advantages of this method it was 1907 before the sinking was completed and the colliery could start full production.

Easington Colliery

In November 1899 the Easington Coal Company began sinking Easington colliery on the deserted cliff tops a mile-and-a-half from the ancient village of Easington. A company of French sinkers was engaged to freeze the shaft but failed. A Belgian company fared no better and the coal company, on the brink of bankruptcy, suspended the sinking. In 1907 the Easington Coal Company was taken over by the Weardale Steel Company. They engaged German engineers to complete the sinking but it was not until 1910 that they had completed the task. As in all things mining luck plays a role. The Easington Coal Company had picked a site where the pressure of the water was particularly ferocious, and to relieve this pressure the sinkers had to construct a third shaft, the West pit, which was sunk to the limestone bed, from which a dump drift was driven to the beach to drain water into the sea.

In 1890, three miles south of Easington, Horden

Sinkers Blackhall colliery, 1908

Collieries Limited sank a pit that was to become the largest pit in Britain. To negotiate the sand feeder they used a new innovation. Instead of freezing the shaft they employed the 'cementation process'. Holes were drilled around the shaft area and cement was injected into these bore holes; this filled the fishers and when set held the water at bay.

While new collieries were being sunk disaster struck at Wingate colliery in 1906, and 24 miners perished when the pit exploded.

Mr P. Bentham of Wingate was 13 years old at the time, and later recalled that the explosion was,

'a very serious blow to the village. There was one particular thing that stuck in my mind. As they were bringing the dead bodies out of the pit there was a whole line of people leaving just sufficient room for the stretcher bearers and the stretchers to get through the crowds. I was standing very close. We could only see the boots of the victims as they were covered from head to foot with a blanket. Several had been carried past and when this particular one was passing a lady standing next to me, immediately on my left, recognised the boots. She collapsed. She knew by the boots it was her husband.'

In October 1909 the Horden Coal Company sank Blackhall Colliery, which was the last of the pits sunk in this phase of development.

Barry Chambers, who became the Lodge Secretary at Blackhall many years later, explained:

Ralph Lee, Survivor of Wingate pit explosion, 1906

Wingate colliery disaster 1906, waiting for news

'When Horden collieries first started they took the Royalties of the Castle Eden 'take' along with Shotton colliery. To de-water Castle Eden colliery they intended sinking a shaft to the east of the colliery but instead they decided to sink a new colliery at Blackhall. Originally the Blackhall colliery was going to be called Castle Eden New Winning. The money they got from the coal from Shotton colliery paid for the Blackhall sinking.

'After they sunk the colliery they started to drive south and hit a fault which threw all the seams upward to about the height of the seam above. They decided to drift west into the Castle Eden workings and built channels to take the water to Blackhall where they built massive pumps to de-water the Castle Eden workings. This was in the 1920s and in 1926 men were given dispensation to stay at work to keep the pumps going. They were able to re-enter the Castle Eden workings about 1928. Then in the thirties there was no demand for coal so the plans to reopen the pit were shelved. Even when I was going to school in the 1950s the teachers were still talking about the pit reopening but by that time Blackhall workings surrounded Castle Eden and there was no point in reopening the colliery. But they had a very lucrative deal with the water board to supply them with fresh water.'

New pits require miners and miners required housing. At Dawdon Londonderry built 20 streets of houses. These new houses were brick-built, double-walled dwellings, many having gardens. Bathrooms and running water were not yet regarded as a priority but these new houses were twentieth-century houses and not the dirt-floored dwellings of the 1840s.

Similarly at Easington red-bricked pit terraces were replacing the green fields. Houses were built tight around the pit-head so the clank of steel against steel, the whistle of steam, and the acrid smell of the furnaces formed the inescapable backdrop of village life.

Houses so close to the pit had their dangers. as Tom Garside knew. Tom was born in 1906 in Kello and moved with his parents to Easington colliery in January 1913.

'I always slept with my brother Alf, and we lived down as what's known as Charles Street, That's the first street east facing the pit, Official Street was not there then. This Monday morning there was a terrible thud as if it was a bracket of thunder, all of a sudden the ceiling came in on top of us lying in bed,

Blackhill Road, Horden

well we were suffering from shock and we found out when we got up, the cage had overshot the landing and dislodged two pieces of girder. One went under the window sill of the house next door, the other one came down one side of the partition on the bed, where two men slept who had gone to work on the early shift. If the girders had gone four feet the other way, me and my brother would have maybe's lost our lives.'

At Horden and Blackhall the terraces when erected were numbered rather than named. After all there was as yet no one to name them after. Unlike Seaham there was no feudal lord to honour, only anonymous coal companies born out of capital raised in far-off places. No leaders of the community — as yet no community. But the streets and houses were soon to fill with families from Wales, Scotland and Ireland. The majority, of course, came from Durham, many from West Durham seeking deliverance from the wet, thin seams of the Pennine foothills.

Klondyke

Typical of the men who made their way to this new Klondyke was Dick Lawson, who had begun his working life at a pit in Whitehaven at the age of 12. In 1891 the family had moved to Boldon colliery. Dick worked at Hylton colliery before moving to Dawdon, where he was elected checkweighmen and in 1908 became the first Lodge Secretary. He was the brother of Jack Lawson, who was MP for Chester-le-Street for many years. The DMA was now well established in the coalfield with a membership of 166,000 miners. In 1880 they negotiated a working shift of no longer than seven-and-a-half hours for hewers and obtained the agreement of the coalowners that a colliery would not raise coal for more than ten or in some cases 11 hours per day. Of course the back-bye, datal hands, who serviced the coal-getting shifts, continued to work long shifts of up to 12 hours.

1908 Act

In 1908 an Act of Parliament restricted the hours of all regular shifts underground to eight hours. This was to have a dramatic affect on the lives of Durham miners. To maximise coal output new shift patterns had to be introduced and the owners responded with three- and in some cases four-shift working over a 24-hour period. Miners were enraged.

Detemined to resist, the Murton miners struck work on 1 January 1910. Short of coal, the whole village stole from the Pea Heap, a heap of unsaleble small coals. On January 20 the authorities drafted into the village a large body of police, some from as far away as Yorkshire, to bring matters to a head. In the course of the day, after several clashes between villagers and police, the Riot Act was read and considerable damage

Murton miners taking coal from Dalton Flats 1910

was done to the viewer's house and the officials' club.

At Horden the discontent resulted in even greater damage. Miners cut the telephone wires before mounting an attack on the house of the manager, who defended himself with a pistol. As the riot progressed a social club built by the coal company was burned down, causing £11,000 worth of damage.

Discontent was county-wide but gradually

subsided as miners were forced to accept that the new pattern of shift working was now going to be part of their life. It was not just the men who suffered. A mother who had several sons on different shifts would have to spread her working day over 24 hours, drying pit clothes and making up bait.

The new shift system transformed the new East Durham pits into huge coal machines turning millions of tons a year on to the market. Dawdon alone was producing a million tons of coal a year and employing 3,300 men. The essential bedrock of East Durham's economy which was to endure for the greater part of the 20 th century was now in place.

1912 saw coal production from the Durham coalfield at its height. Britain, not yet weakened by World Wars, was at the peak of its manufacturing power. Coal was the sole source of energy. Oil was as yet not a serious rival. It was coal which bunkered the sea-going vessels, powered the extensive network of railways, provided gas and steam power for the factories, and heated homes.

In 1908 the Durham Miners Association under pressure from the membership and against the wishes of its General Secretary, John Wilson, rejoined the Miners Federation of Great Britain (MFGB). Now all British miners were united in one union. Now was the time to start to redress the main grievances.

The MFGB turned its attention to the question of a minimum wage.

The greater part of coal produced was still hewed by the brute force of the hewers, who were paid by the amount of coal they produced. If the going was good, the seam dry and the coal soft, wages were, if not generous, adequate. The marginal benefits of free housing and free fire-coal made British miners the best-paid in Europe. But if the coal was hard, the roof weak and the floor running in water, the rewards could be less than what was necessary to sustain life.

In October 1911 the MFGB carried a resolution calling for a National Minimum Wage, and in February 1912 a national strike was called. Within days the country was at a virtual standstill. Never had the miners of Britain been in a better position to assert their authority. Never had their cause been more just.

The Government, realising the strength of the miners, rushed a Bill through Parliament making provision for a minimum wage to be negotiated at local level.

Many of the miners' leaders recognised that if the

minimum was negotiated on a regional basis this would undermine the collective strength of the Federation. What they wanted was a National Minimum which would bind the miners together as a national body. The Federation leaders, however, prevaricated and in April when a ballot was held failed to give a recommendation to accept the offer or continue with the strike. The ballot rejected the offer but failed to secure a two-thirds majority to continue the strike, so that only a partial victory was achieved - a minimum wage to be negotiated at County level..

In Durham the Executive Committee ordered a resumption of work without consulting the membership and narrowly escaped a vote of no confidence by 302 delegates voting for to 321 against.

Seaham colliery miners' Strike Ccommittee 1922

Times were changing and the union was changing. The old guard who had led the union in the closing decades of the 19th century, men like Foreman, Crawford and Wilson, were a particular breed. They were either from Primitive Methodist families or had converted to Primitive Methodist. Their strength came from deeply held religious conviction. Education, trade unionism, co-operation and sobriety were their watchwords. Working men, they believed could take their rightful place in society through the power of reason.

The Liberal Party had gained a huge electoral advantage by building an alliance with the mining districts in Durham. Candidates from the trade union movement who stood as Liberals were known as Lib-Lab candidates. The Lib-Lab tradition was epitomised by John Wilson, who had been instrumental in establishing a union at Haswell colliery, for which he was victimised and forced for a time to earn his living as a stationer at Wheatley Hill. He found employment again in the industry and became a lodge official and then checkweighman at Wheatley Hill. In 1882 he was elected to the position of County Agent.

In 1885 Wilson became the Liberal MP for Houghton-le-Spring, and after the death of DMA General Secretary William Crawford in 1890 he took over Crawford's seat of Mid-Durham.

John Wilson

Independent Labour Party

Socialist ideas opposed to the philosophy of the DMA leadership had been developing in the coalfield for the last two decades of the 19th century. The most prominent group in Durham was the Independent Labour Party (ILP). The strength of their influence was reflected in the aftermath of the 1912 strike, when they held protest meetings throughout the county that were better attended than the official union meetings.

One leader who lived through the transition from Liberal to Labour politics was Peter Lee.

Peter Lee was born into a family of eight at Duff Heap Row, Five Houses, Trimdon Grange in 1864 and started his working life at Littletown colliery at the age of 10. By the age of 16 he was a hewer and a dedicated devil-may-care drinker, gambler and bare- knuckle fighter.

One day at the age of 19 he was drinking in the Colliery Arms Inn in Wingate when he began to reflect upon the pointless direction of his life and decided to get an education by going to night classes. By 1886, his restive spirit had taken him to no less than thirteen collieries in Durham, Lancashire and Cumberland. In the same year, at the age of 22, he set sail for the USA. His North American adventure was, however, short-lived. After working in the mines of Pittsburgh, Indiana and Kentucky he returned home to take up employment at Wingate Colliery, where he was soon to be elected as the Lodge delegate. After three years he was off on his travels again, this time to South Africa, where he worked in the gold mines. Never able to settle and not able to resist a challenge, he returned to Britain overland via Italy and France.

Home again and aged 33 he made a decision that was to transform his life. He converted to

Peter Lee

Primitive Methodism and became a lay preacher. His conversion to the Primitives fitted in exactly with the model of a miners' leader of the day — Methodist, self-taught and a Liberal. By 1903 he was the checkweighman at Wheatley Hill and in the same year was elected to the position of Chairman of the Parish Council, and led a crusade against the insanitary conditions in the local pit villages, championing the cause of household running water, street lighting and village drains.

In the 1900 conference of the TUC, the MFGB voted against the formation of the Labour Representation Committee and in 1906 refused to join the newly formed Labour Party. The matter was not resolved untill 1908, when the MFGB agreed to become a part of the new party based on the Trade Unions.

Up to 1908 the DMA, and particularly its leader John Wilson, was still committed to an alliance with the Liberal Party. But when in 1908 the DMA joined the MFGB they were bound by the collective decision of the British miners to support the Labour Party. The transformation in Durham was both rapid and universal. This seismic shift in the political landscape reverberated through the ranks of the DMA. John Wilson was never to reconcile himself to Labour Party membership but Peter Lee embraced the new politics with enthusiasm. In 1909 he was elected as one of the first 10 Labour members to the Durham County Council (DCC). Ten years later he became the first Labour Party Chaiman of the DCC, making him effectively the centre of County Durham Society.

The Labour Party was a 'broad church', a coalition of small socialist organisations in alliance with the trade unions Of these socialist groups the one which was to have the greatest influence on the DMA and the life of East Durham was the Independent Labour Party (ILP), which was established in 1893. It became most influential amongst checkweighmen and was dominated by Primitive Methodists who translated their strong religious views into a political philosophy through the medium of the ILP. To counter Wilson's opposition to the Labour Representation Committee they had formed a County rank-and-file association called the 'Labour Council' to pressure the DMA into breaking from the Liberal Party.

One of its young activists was Edward Cain. Edward was the son of a West of Ireland Catholic immigrant and a Scottish Protestant mother. This unlikely union produced a very stormy family life. His father, a gentle man when sober, was a devil in drink. His mother was long-suffering and heroic in the defence of her children. In Edward's earliy life the family trailed from one pit to another. They experienced rough lodgings and hard times. He later recalled that:

'The work at Shotton came to an end in 1911 on 4th of April when Dad got 14 days notice to leave the colliery house and the colliery. Brother Tom and I had not lost any time, but were included in the notice. I decided to ask the union to deal with our case. The union dealt with the matter and Alderman William House, agent for the D.M.A., was successful in getting Tom and I two weeks wages for wrongful dismissal.

'I had been active in the I.L.P. and attending meetings for some time, and I was interested in the book of William Morris, News from Nowhere, Blatchford's Merrie England,

Zeppelin over railway street Seaham during First World War

Bruce Glasier's Meaning of Socialism, Tom Paine's Rights of Man and The Age of Reason and many other books. I was now a bit of a rebel. After searching for work for over a week, we finally got started at Wheatley Hill and on 11th April, 1911, we moved again into a new house in 15th Street, Wheatley Hill.'

William House was the first DMA agent to be a member of the ILP. But not all union men were as keen to help. Edwards recalled:

'Mr Peter Lee objected to us having the use of a room in the Miners' Hall for our [ILP] meetings. We had therefore to have our meetings in members' homes'

Peter Lee had made the transformation from Liberal to Labour but never embraced the more 'Marxist' ILP.

With the start of the First World War in 1914 the pits of East Durham were brought under state control by the Liberal Government of Lloyd George, a move warmly accepted by the miners' union. The mining industry in the hands of the private owners had become increasingly chaotic and backward. Compared with the rest of the industry the collieries of East Durham were beacons of efficiency and large-scale production. The war effort strengthened their position as premier producers. The effect of state control benefitted the less efficient owners, who were subsidised by the profits from the more efficient collieries. All owners prospered and by 1918 profits had trebled.

Many of East Durham miners left the pits in the early months of the war and perished in the subsequent carnage. Those who remained faced the dangers of the pits.

For Tom Garside, not yet old enough to work, life had its lighter moments.

'I can remember in June or July in 1913 when there was crowds around the banks down the beach, I don't know whether it was a publicity stunt, some say it was Houdini. There was a boat on the beach, this man was put in a straight jacket, handcuffed, chains put around him, they took him out about 20 yards at sea, and threw him into the sea, and after a few seconds he came back up.

'We watched the bombardment of Hartlepool in 1914 in December. They brought all the men out of the pit. It was a hazy day, you couldn't see no ships, all you heard was a clatter and an echo. You could see the black smoke lifting on the sea front at Hartlepool. You couldn't see far out at sea because it was a bright sunny morning, but you could see along the coast.

'We were standing on top of the coal houses, the officials' houses were up then in 1915. And we could see right along from there, we got a good view. After that, I went for my holidays at Kelloe, where I had come from. It was bombed by a Zeppelin.

'I can remember in 1917 we were down the dene getting nuts when a submarine bobbed up about a mile off Easington viaduct and bombarded Seaham and Dawdon. At that particular time there was troops under canvas and they must have known they were there. We could see three or four come up onto the gun on the submarine and the tower where the officers were in, and they fired about six or seven rounds at the cooling tower'.

Chapter 4

Group of miners outside Royal Hotel, Third Street, Horden 1920

At the end of the first World War, when the promised 'land fit for heroes' did not materialise, Edward Cain saw the need for political action and the building of a strong Labour Party. On November 14 1914 he had joined the Royal Garrison Artillery and had arrived on the 6th of December in Newhaven, where he was vaccinated. He had an advese reaction to the vaccination and was hospitalised and later contracted glandular fever, which kept him inactive for some considerable time. He told an interviewer in 1976:

'At the end of the 1914-1918 War, the need for a Labour Party was evident and the union officials were not yet keen on the ILP, but in December 1918, Major Hayward (Liberal) defeated Mr J Lawson (Labour). The election work was done in the main by members of the ILP, the union officials, not being politically minded, although Peter Lee, who had been a Liberal, came over to the Labour Party, but was never a member of the ILP.

'In the spring of 1919 a meeting was convened in Murton Miners Hall, to form a Labour Party in the East Durham Division. The following were present: Joe Blackwell, George Bloomfield, E Cain, The Rev. Jack Heron, Peter Lee and George Walker.

A vacancy occurred in the Chester-le-Street Division, and Jack Lawson left the East Durham Division and went to Chester-Le-Street, which he contested and won, and held the seat until his death. The I.L.P. was now more active than ever, bringing speakers every week to the Division'.

In the post-war years the Labour Party grew in influence and achieved in Durham a dominance unrivalled anywhere in the country. The economy of East Durham was coal and the politics Labour. The two were indivisible.

The first post-war days were full of optimism. The mines were still under state control but the Government was making moves to hand control back to the owners. In 1919 the MFGB demanded a 30 per cent advance in wages and the members voted by a large majority to strike. In a ploy to avert the strike the Government set up a committee under the chairmanship of Justice Sankey to make recommendations on the level of wages, the hours of work and the method of control of the industry. The committee consisted of representatives of the mine-owners, the MFGB, and six independent capitalists. Of the six representatives of the MFGB only three were union officials, the other three were experts nominated by the union. Most prominent of these was Sydney Webb.

Sankey Commission

The Sankey Commission recommended a two shillings per shift advance in wages and a reduction in the working day for all underground miners from eight to seven hours. They also gave a somewhat vague recommendation that the industry be nationalised. The Government agreed to honour the recommendation on hours and wages and the MFGB gratefully accepted the offer. Sydney Webb was widely regarded as the chief architect of the victory.

Sydney Webb was a lecturer in economics and a prominent member of the Fabians. The Fabian socialists represented the moderate wing of the Labour Party, taking their name from the Roman General Fabian, whose military strategy consisted of continuous tactical retreats. Webb's passion was industrial efficiency, and in the hearings of the Sankey Commission he had mercilessly exposed the inefficiency of the coal-owners, and won the respect of the mining communities. The community of Seaham Harbour was no exception, and the local Labour Party was determined to have him as its prospective parliamentary candidate.

The Seaham Labour Party had won the District Council elections of 1919. The chairman of the Party was Robert Broad, checkweighman at Dawdon colliery.

The nomination of Sydney Webb as Labour candidate for Seaham was not without opposition. To succeed Webb had to leap-frog other hopefuls who were already on the DMA's list of approved parliamentary candidates. The Durham Executive Committee vetoed Webb's nomination and Webb accepted their decision. The Seaham Labour Party members were however very determined, and persuaded Webb to abide by the decision of the local Labour Party. On July 20 1920 he accepted the nomination. Webb secured the agreement of the local party that he would not be required to live in the constituency and that his constituency duties would be minimal.

In 1922 Webb was elected the Labour MP for Seaham Harbour with a majoriity of 10,624 votes, much to the annoyance and consternation of Lord Londonderry. To

bring to his town founded on private enterprise the tormentor from the Sankey commission and advocate of nationalisation was to add insult to injury.

Industrial peace, however, did not last long. In 1921 control of the mines was handed back to the

Group of South Hetton colliery fitters, 1920

owners. The owners immediately anounced wage cuts and when the miners refused to accept them they were locked out in April of that year.

Tom Garside was now a youth of 15 and working as a miner at Easington coliery. He remembered that,

'The 1921 strike only lasted a few weeks. The engines at the pits were driven by steam in those days and they were short of coal at the colliery, so the officials had to go down the pit and hew coal. One day, two twenty- ton trucks were filled and they lowered them down the colliery sidings to Fairs Bridge, then the officials went for their dinners. After about an hour when they came back, the trucks were still there, but they were empty, the strikers had opened the bottoms of the trucks and they were running away with tin-baths full of coal, and they carried all the coal away.

'The manager, they called him Mr Robinson, sent for the secretary of the union, Mr Bloomfield. The manager explained to him what had happened so the secretary of the union said, 'What's that got to do with me'?.

The manager said "You are secretary of the union, aren't you?"

'"Yes" replied Mr Bloomfield, "But I am not secretary of the whole village"

'There was no dole, no nothing in those days. You had to tick on for something to eat. You had to depend upon the stores, or the shopkeepers, and pay it back later on, you could not go for National Assistance unless there was somebody sick in the family, then they would give maybe's a voucher for £1 and you would have to go to Walter Wilson's and buy groceries with it'.

Britain, weakened by the huge burden of debt, fell on hard times. Coal production, which had peaked in 1913, was now in decline. East Durham only escaped the worst effects of the downturn in trade due to the relatively modern state of its mines. While the more antiquated pits in the West of the coalfield faced closure the East was even increasing its capacity.

In July 1924 an agreement was drawn up between the Londonderry collieries and two Belgian firms which specialised in shaft sinking to act as joint contractors and sink new shafts through the permian strata to the north of Seaham Harbour just 250 yards from the sea.

The new shafts were sunk 200 yards apart with a fiinshed shaft diameter of 21 ft. The shafts were named the Vane and the Tempest respectively and the colliery was first called the New Seaham colliery, but became known as Vane Tempest colliery.

It was now a century since the first shaft was successfully sunk through the limestone, but the power of the sand feeder was undiminished. Mining technique was however well established,

Freezing opperation at Vane Tempest colliery 1925

and to emasculate the power of the water was only a matter of cost.

On September 18 1925 the sinkers began freezing the Tempest shaft, and by January 21 1926 an ice wall had formed around the shaft area sufficient to hold the water at bay. On February 16 1926 the excavation of the shaft began and by May 1 a depth of 280 ft had been reached. This was as deep as the shaft would get for some time as this was the day the General Strike began.

Edward Cain had spent the previous years, like many of the 'political miners', engrossed in self-education. He had met a mentor, a Mr. Bob Smith, who 'proved to be a teacher and a friend'.

'My education in my boyhood had been little, but under the supervision of Mr Smith, not only did I learn mathematics, but I sat an exam at Ryhope and passed as a Deputy Overman. Mr. Smith was also a man of music and soon I had a violin, and he soon had me playing in the Wheatley Hill Orchestra, conducted by another keen musician, Bob Walker. I was now playing in churches and chapels all over the district.

'In 1922 I was elected Chairman of the Wheatley Hill Miner's Lodge, and held the post until July, 1930. In 1925, the coalowners issued a notice to the miners, that unless they were willing to take a reduction in wages, and work an hour longer, the pits would close. The Miners Federation of Great Britain refused this demand and in May 1926 the whole of the miners in Great Britain were locked out. Realising the seriousness of the situation, a special meeting of the miners' lodge at Wheatley Hill was called to form various committees, there was a committee for feeding the children, and despatch riders were organised due to cancellation of traffic.

'To cover the steady working of the whole system, a council of action was formed on 6th April, 1926. The Independent Labour Party Committee organised pickets for various points such as Vincent's Corner, Colliery

Office, Patton Street, and credit was arranged with tradesmen to help members during the stoppage.

'On learning that a United Service bus was running to break the strike, the pickets assembled at Thornley Crossings, and when the bus appeared it was met with a hurricane of stones that shattered the glass windows. There were no more bus rides following this. On another occasion at the top of the road, East View, when it was known that a bus load of police were on their way to Wheatley Hill, the pickets put a telegraph pole and other obstacles across the road.

'The police got out of the bus and rushed to clear the road and some of the pickets got in the way. The police then rushed the crowd who were standing by and four men were arrested and tried at Castle Eden Police Court then fined £50 or five months imprisonment each. They were Messrs. J Cain, M Ruth, G Carpenter, and W Holland. The miners lodge was affiliated to the Red International Labour Union (R.I.L.U) who immediately paid the fines.

'Eventually, the coal stoppage came to an end and it was soon evident that the Manager was not going to re-employ me, despite my repeated visits to the office. I was living in a colliery house and an eviction order was given for my removal, along with three others. I was given a Council house, 16 Byron Street. I again approached the Manager at the colliery for work, but the answer I got was, "If you give up your ideas of Socialism you can start".

I refused to do so. I visited several collieries for work, without success.

'Then I was given eighteen weeks work, road making, at Town Kelloe, following this I had another long spell on the dole. Another eighteen weeks spell making the footpath by the "Gassy gutter" between Wheatley Hill and Thornley, and making the footpath on the Quarry Road. This was the only work I had from 1926 until Wingate colliery closed in June 1930, when I was appointed by Mr J.A. Stewart, Manager of the Wingate Labour Exchange, to work as a clerk in his department.

'I worked there until the beginning of January, 1934, when I commenced as checkweighman with William Lawther at Wheatley Hill Colliery. Upon my return to the colliery, I was elected secretary to the Miners' Lodge, there I spent a great deal of time looking after the unemployed'

Edwards' experience was typical.

Tom Garside recalls some lighter moments:

'1926, was a good summer, right away up to November the weather was lovely. In them days AJ Cook was General Secretary of the union and when he used to come into the area they used to get the band out. He was at Ryhope and Rainton, and different places and I used to help by carrying the band's instruments. We used to march in and hear him speak. We also used to go to Shotton Pit heap and collect dust. We put it in water and

Soup kitchen, Blackhall, 1926

made balls with it and let them dry out for the fire, we used them for our coal. We used to rake about the sidings at the colliery down here, looking for coal and the police used to chase us. I can remember one time, I was talking to a man belonging to Horden, and he said "Why not go to the tip on beach down Warren House." So two or three of us decided to go down this morning at about 4.a.m. Well, we goes to Horden with our boneshakers. Well we were just about to go up to the tip, when this bloke popped out of a hole he had made

at the top of the heap, and he started to throw stones down at us. So we went away and went back later, the same thing happened, and we found out that this man had gone mental and he was taken to the asylum, so we didn't go there any more.

'We used to have different kinds of sports, there was pit pony racing, there was about 80 or 90 ponies at the colliery in them days, and they were in the fields grazing, and we used to pick the best out of them and take them round to the Welfare Park. The local bookmakers used to be there, you could have a bet on the horses, if you had any money.

'The clubs used to organize them. In those days we had the Comrades Club, that's where the Central Club is now, and they used to organize a lot of things like that. We used to have tip-top speakers. Saclatvalus and different M.P.'s used to come out to speak to us. But our M.P. was Sidney Webb and he used to come out. You always had something to occupy your time, but the food was a problem but you just had to make the best of it. It is marvellous how you survive when you have to'.

Life was hard before the strike and harder during the strike. The burden of managing the meagre rations fell on the women. Their life centred around the kitchen in an endless routine of cooking, cleaning and raising children. Testimony to their labours is the fond memories many had of a childhood in the 20's.

Inner Dock, Seaham Harbour

Adeline Hodges grew up in Dawdon. In later years she reflected on a happy childhood spent in poverty:

'My childhood was spent in a world of contentment for we longed for nothing we could not have, moreover we were all in the same boat. The tuck shops only sold what was within our means to buy and one could not outclass another.

'But we knew dire poverty when the big strike came. Mother had bought plenty of flour in readiness because she said you could manage with plenty of bread. But alas! The mice got into the sacks. I always laugh now at the advertisement about "the graded grains make finer flour". I picture us with sheets of clean paper spread everywhere, sifting the mouse dirt from the flour, because mother could not afford to waste it. It nearly broke her heart, but father always cheerful said, "Never mind, the thicker the meat, the stronger the man"'.

Many miners lived off the land rabbiting and fishing. Mr G. Cole was five years old when he came with his father to Seaham in 1901 from Yorkshire. In 1926 he was working as an onsetter at Seaham colliery. His memory of the 1926 strike was almost idyllic:

'In Seaham Harbour the bulk of the men spent their time fishing. At that time no one was allowed on the North Pier, because after it was built there was a storm and all the iron railings were washed off. I've heard men say that there has not been so many fish caught before or since. About five o clock at night a lot of men would go down there and you could not get a seat on the Pier. You would think the Lord was on their side, the whities came in and were giving themselves up.

'The weather was really good and everyone was down bathing. I remember once when we were down watching them bathing, I saw a well dressed man. The fellow said, "Well they reckon we'll beat them, but they'll never beat people with morale like this"'.

Durham had stayed out on strike longer than any other coalfield. Prior to the strike hewers' hours in Durham were shorter than those in other coalfields, and in some cases they were working only six-and-a-half hours bank to bank. To increase this to eight hours was a massive change and they resisted right up to the end. The final ballot held on November 1926 still achieved a majority to continue the strike but failed to gain the two-thirds majority required by the DMA rules. One concession was wrested from the owners: the hewers' hours in Durham were increased to seven-and-a-half while in the rest of the country it was eight.

If the strike itself was hard the aftermath was unbearable as the coal industry lunged into recession and the owners imposed more and more reductions. Again the East Durham pits faired better than the older collieries in the West, many of which failed to restart production after 1926.

In contrast, work on the second shaft, the Vane, began on May 18 1927 at Londonderry's new pit. The sinkers blasted their way through the limestone and frozen sand at a speed that would have amazed the early sinkers. In all it took 83 and-a-half days to reach the finished depth of 606 ft., an average of 7 ft. per day. The Dawdon sinkers 27 years before had only achieved 11 inches per day through the frozen ground.

Despite the crushing defeat the East coast miners were robust in resisting further reductions. Wages

James Ancram

in the East were consistently above the county average and in 1929 4,000 Dawdon miners were locked out from March until June when they refused to accept a wage reduction.

The dispute made Seaham Harbour a hotbed of political action and attracted to the village a number of well known politiical activists from the Communist Party. James Ancram, a communist Councillor from Felling, Gateshead, had organised a soup kitchen on behalf of the Workers International Relief committee. George Lumley, the communist checkweighman from Ryhope colliery, was a regular visitor, as was Harry Pollitt, the leader of the British Communist Party.

In 1929 Sydney Webb gave notice that he wished to resign his seat at the next General Election, due to take place in November of that year. Webb conspired with Arthur Henderson, the National Chairman of the Labour Party and director of Newcastle Football Club, to secure the seat for Ramsay MacDonald, leader of the Labour Party. MacDonald, like Webb before him, would not be required either to live in the community or to have any constituency duties.

Webb was good enough to warn MacDonald that if he took the seat he should be sure to keep his friendship with Lord Londonderry a secret, for obvious reasons.

In the election of 1929 Ramsay MacDonald secured the seat with a majority of 28,794, while Harry Pollitt for the Communist Party and the Liberal candidate lost their deposits.

The Labour Party emerged from the 1929 election as the biggest Parliamentary Party but without an overall majority, and took office for the second time in the decade dependent upon the support of the Liberals.

MacDonald, however, continued his friendship with Londonderry and was a frequent visitor to Wynyard Hall. It could be said that he abused the Lord's friendship as he had an affair with Lady Londonderry and wrote her love letters. The letters were addressed 'Dear Circe', the name of the Greek goddess who set men's hearts aflame, and signed 'Hamish the Hunter'.

Jimmy Maxton, the left-wing Clydeside MP, was

Ramsay McDonald opening aged Miners cottages at Murton

known to say jokingly that the Labour Party should change its anthem from the Red Flag to the Londonderry Air.

MacDonald was no stranger to scandal. His assignations with a French woman got him in trouble but the establishment came to his aid when the Foreign Office paid £10,000 to keep the affair out of the press. A much bigger scandal was about to break with devastating consequences for the Labour movement and Seaham in particular.

MacDonald had been elected on the slogan 'Full work or full maintenance'. As the effects of the 1929 Wall Street crash plunged the British economy deeper into slump the City bankers demanded Government action. In 1931 MacDonald introduced the hated Means Test and cut the dole, splitting the Cabinet. The Government resigned and MacDonald was asked by King George V to form a National Government consisting mainly of Tories.

In the subsequent General Election in 1931 MacDonald stood against the Labour candidate in Seaham and was elected with a reduced majority of 6,000. Between 1931 and 1935 MacDonald was only seen in his Seaham constituency twice, and in the election campaign of 1935 he was subjected to universal derision from the population.

MacDonald had the advantage of resources, and a temporary air strip was constructed at Shotton to ferry his supporters from London into the constituency. But MacDonald's time had run out. The local Labour Party had had time to recover from MacDonald's betrayal, and stood Emanuel Shinwell, who easily defeated the now hated MacDonald.

The Great Depression of the 30s had an immediate effect in East Durham. The older pits were the most vulnerable. By June 1930 2,000 men and boys were paid off at Shotton colliery. In October of the same year Seaham and Trimdon Grange collieries closed down temporarily, throwing more miners on to the dole. In May 1924 172,026 miners were employed in Durham's collieries. By December 1931 this figure had plummeted to 107,938, many of whom were on short-time working. No colliery, however efficient, avoided the slump in the export trade. Londonderry collieries dismissed 2,600 men between 1931 and 1932.

The whole of East Durham was now plunged into depression. The lives of those miners lucky enough to be working was dominated by the pit buzzer which signalled to the community which seams would be worked the next day. Unless they had three consecutive days without employment they did not qualify for relief.

The seventh Marquis of Londonderry was having a better time. In 1931 his old friend MacDonald appointed him Secretary of State for Air, a post which he kept until 1935. Counted among Londonderry's friends were Hitler, Goering, Von Neurath and Ribbentrop. He was a frequent visitor to Hitler and in 1938 he wrote a Penguin Special arguing for a sympathetic view of the German dictator, arguing that Britain should ' extend the hand of true friendship to the Third Reich'.

Hitler was more than pleased with his friend and on April 10 1930 wrote:

Dear Lord Londonderry,

I have received with great interest your recent book *Ourselves and Germany* which you have just sent to me, with an inscription written in your own hand. I share with you the hope of a better understanding between our two countries which you have thus expressed.

Please accept my warmest thanks for this renewed and valued notice of my work, as well as the appreciation shown in your book.

With my best regards to Lady Londonderry and with friendly greetings,

Yours cordially.

Adolf Hitler

Tom Garside was one of the miners paid off from Easington colliery when a seam was closed in 1933:

' The coal, they wanted a certain class of coal, they didn't want steam coal because the ships had changed over from coal to diesel and this Main Coal seam produced steam coal, what the ships used to use, so they closed the Main Coal seam. In them days, you had to wait so long and then you got a green card and you got 16 weeks work. I remember I got this job at Easington Village. They wanted 22 ft. cut off the cemetery to widen the road. On the Hetton road, where the Mason's Arms is now and practically all the men that was working on there were miners. They were like myself unemployed through the closure of the Main Coal. We worked at night time and it was all screened off from the public. We removed the wall and we removed about 80 or 90 of the Haswell miners who were buried there. They were all in single file, and we broke into four or five tombs and I can remember one girl whose skull and hair were perfect. Black hair she had, and two students came from Durham University and took the skull and hair away with them.

'Then after that job finished, there was no work again. So I just knocked around, started bookmaking, then I started tic-tacking on the dog tracks. They opened the dog track out at Easington Village and I was doing quite well, till the war broke out, so it either meant going in the forces, or back to the pits, so I decided to go back to the pits.'

Seaham banner at Durham Miners Gala, 1930

Chapter 5

Women's Auxiliaries, Seaham 1937

Despite Londonderry's best efforts war with Germany was declared in 1939.

Coal production for the war effort was slow to start. In September 1939 there were 18,372 miners unemployed in Durham. By December of that year the figure had been reduced only to 15,087, and in March 1940 6,571 were still unemployed.

The most immediate affect of the war was the disruption of the all-important shipping link between Durham and London. Efforts to send more coal by rail were frustrated by the bad weather.

Reluctantly miners agreed to double-shift working and the suspension of statutory holidays to boost production. However, the difficulties of transporting the coal out of the region and the loss of markets on the continent meant that the increased production led to short-time working and unemployment. Such was the crisis that the DMA toured other coalfields to see if it was viable to resettle Durham miners there. In this initial phase of the war many working and unemployed miners volunteered to join the army, and for the second time in 25 years miners were exchanging their picks for rifles.

Unrest

By March 1940 16,000 miners either found new jobs or joined the army. This loss of so many younger and fitter miners had its effect upon production. An older workforce, inadequate food and low wages sapped morale, and when it became clear that men and women working in munitions were earning higher wages than datal workers working six shifts a week unrest was inevitable.

In May 1941 the government introduced the Essential Works Order, making coalmining a reserved occupation. For the first time since the bond was abolished in 1872 miners were legally tied to the colliery where they worked. Under these powers it became a criminal offence to strike or to be absent from work for any reason other than certified sickness.

On June 26 1942 13 men died in an explosion in the Five Quarter Back Over flat at Murton colliery. The tragedy was caused by the use of the wrong type of shot-firing equipment by the deputy. Steve Cummings was an overman at the colliery and a member of the local rescue brigade. He later wrote:

'At 6.30 on Friday June 26 I was at my home completing the summary of the weekly wages of the men and boys under my supervision at the colliery. I received an urgent message from the colliery to report at once to the colliery rescue and ambulance centre as there had been an explosion at the mine. I felt stunned, and failed to ask where [the explosion had occurred]. In my mind's eye was my district where approximately 70 to 80 men and boys were underground at the time....

'I pulled on a pair of heavy boots and boiler suit and made my way to report for duty, being one of the six trained Fire and Rescue workers at the colliery under the organisation of the Durham and Northumberland Fire and Rescue Brigade. Fifty yards from home I met a workman coming from the colliery and asked [him] where the trouble had occurred. It was really a little relief when he said, "the Backover Flat", knowing that only about 15 men worked this unit'.

The war did not eliminate the miners' sense of grievance at having to undergo such dangers for so little reward.

In 1943 3,000 men at Horden colliery took strike action in support of the datal hands, who were demanding better conditions. The strike spread to Blackhall colliery before it was resolved, and in January 1944 Easington colliery was on strike for a week for higher wages.

This was the first war in which the lives of civilians were seriously threatened. The coastal

Miners' Lodge Officials and Manager, Deaf Hill, Vesting Day 1947

collieries were a regular target for enemy bombers and given the close proximity of the colliery rows no one was safe. The nightly routine of sleeping in the air-raid shelter or under the stairs did nothing to make life easier. By 1945 everyone was ready for a change, and the biggest change that could take place was in the running of the country. The massive mandate given to the post-war Labour Government was celebrated in East Durham with enthusiasm. At last there was something to look forward to. When the local MP, Emanuel Shinwell, was made the Minister of Fuel and Power with a mandate to nationalise the industry there were real grounds for optimism. With a prospect of an industry 'managed for and behalf of the people' the future had to be bright. And so it was.

After vesting day in 1947 the country was hit by a coal crisis and miners were asked to be patient and not demand the five-day week which they had been promised. Wages rose and the new management began a programme of modernisation. For the first time the collieries in the West were able to afford the luxury of pit-head baths. The coastal collieries were to receive the largest injection of capital in their history.

Easington Explosion

Work began at Easington in 1951 on a modernisation program which was to transform

Emanual Shinwell MP

production at the colliery. It was, however, tragically halted when on May 29 of that year the Duckbill District in the North Pit's Five Quarter seam exploded, killing 81 men almost instantaneously. Two more, members of the Rescue Brigade, were to perish in the attempt to enter the stricken district. Until now the new pits on the East coast had all escaped major disaster. Although men had been killed in their ones and

Dawdon miners' retirement presentation 1953

twos nothing approaching the scale of this disaster had ever occurred. The community was devastated, the more so in that it had happened just when great changes for the better were taking place. Some would speculate that it was precisely the more relaxed atmosphere between management and unions which allowed a situation to occur where men continued to work in a district where the level of gas emissions was clearly dangerous.

All collieries on the coast benefited from the modernisation programme, which introduced horizon mining into the collieries. Two-ton mine cars replaced the old 10 cwt. tubs underground; locomotives replaced the main and tail haulers, and coal was brought to bank in massive skips and transported to modern washing plants by conveyor belts.

At Murton colliery a new shaft was sunk just west

Bllackhall colliery

of Hawthorn village to draw the coal from Murton, Eppleton and South Hetton collieries which were linked underground, creating the largest mining complex in Europe. A new coking plant, washery and chemical products works were built on the site next to the new shaft.

Barry Chambers started work at Blackhall colliery in 1957. He represented a new breed of miners unaffected by the strikes, lockouts and depression of the 20s and 30s. He started work at a time of optimism in a nationalised industry which promised to train him and look after him for life. After completing his basic training he started work underground as a driver. He recalls:

'Blackhall colliery was one of the first to have skip winding installed in 1956 and the reconstruction was done in stages. The South

shaft drew all the coal from the North pit workings in the Hutton and Low Main. The South pit workings were still bord and pillar and the coal from those workings was drawn at the North pit. So the coal from the South workings was drawn in tubs right up until 1967. The workings were very extensive at that time; there would be men working underground at Blackhall up to nine miles apart. The West Hutton seam was worked until about 1974 and it was under Shotton and you had the East Low Main which was working five miles out-bye under the sea.

'Castle Eden colliery was always an integral part of Blackhall. Although we were connected underground we had men working there, manning the pumps. We had to skirt round the Castle Eden workings and sometimes go underneath to get up to the Shotton workings, so it was a very complex operation on the West side.'

The pits were not the only place to see changes. The post-war years were the years of social engineering and the North-east was not to be an exception. The planning department thoughts turned towards the problem of housing. The old pit houses built when the older pits were sunk were by the 20s well past their 'sell-by date'. In fact they had never been of an acceptable standard.

Despite the desperate times the new Labour Council did its best to clear the worst of the colliery slums and replace them with council houses. Much of Murton's old colliery rows had been cleared before the war. The planners were confronted with a dual problem. The colliery housing stock around the newer collieries in the East, while not of the highest standard, were tolerable and capable of modernisation. The area however suffered from gross overcrowding. The housing stock to the West in the older colliery villages was poor and much could be categorised as slums. The question the planners asked was; if we replace the old houses to the West with modern council houses and the collieries close, then the population will drift to the East and make worse the already existing overcrowding problem. Their solution was to build a new model village close enough to the long-life pits on the East coast and not too far from the older villages. This was thought to be the best strategy to prevent inter-village competition for limited housing resources.

In 1943 the Minister for Health requested all local authorities to asses the housing needs in their localities and devise a long-term plan for post-war redevelopment.

3rd Street Horden

Easington Rural District Council (ERDC) responded in 1946 with a document entitled 'Farewell to Squalor', written by a C.W. Clarke, the Council's Engineer and Surveyor. Clarke has been variously described as idealistic, eccentric and a visionary and his document acclaimed as impressive by his admirers, but his work was referred to as a 'Mein Kampf' by some of his critics. It was Clarke's suggestion that no more fitting name for the new town could be devised than Peterlee, after the the man who first began to oppose the squalor of the pit villages. He concluded his document with the stirring words:

> 'Let us open our eyes and look brightly forward and onward to the new town, the new living ...Peterlee'.

The position of the new town was hotly contested between the two most interested parties: the NCB, jealous of its coal reserves and fearful of high compensation cost for subsidence, and the Ministry of Agriculture, conscious of the loss of agricultural productivity in an economy where food rationing still blighted the lives of ordinary people. Finally a site was agreed to the West of Shotton colliery to the North-west of Horden and to the South of Easington, and the first sod was cut in 1950.

Durham County Council was addressing the problems of the villages throughout the county and was seeking along with national government policy to direct the population towards designated centres where employment could be encouraged. Newton Aycliffe in the west fitted this strategy as did Peterlee in the East. The only difference between them was in the state of the local mining industry. In the West coalmining suffered a catastrophe in the 30s which led to much higher unemployment and depopulation, many emigrating to the more prosperous East. There was a need for opportunities for male employment to be encouraged, whereas around Peterlee the mines

East Front Street, South Hetton

South Hetton fight to stay out of Peterlee, 1959
Photo: Sunderland Echo

were still dependent on large concentrations of male labour and any competing industry was unwelcome.

In order to encourage a shift of population DCC devised a method of allocating resources to the villages by categorising them on a scale from 'A' to 'D'. 'A' were the preferred centres of population and would receive the greatest resources. At the bottom of the pile was 'D': D was for decline and no resources were to be allocated in this category. Those who lived in villages with the D tag were left in no doubt that their only course to better housing was to move, preferably to an A area.

From the start the new town of Peterlee was controversial. The first houses were erected on a site which was barren and windswept and in the long wet winters was a sea of mud. There were no amenities, no entertainment, no shops, no buses, and to cap it all the rents were twice those in the older settlements.

The Peterlee Development Corporation received its finance direct from government and not from rates. Whereas the council could subsidise new-built council housing from the revenue from older housing the new corporations had no such subsidy and had to pay huge interest payments from their only source of revenue, the rents.

South Hetton Resist

It was little wonder that opposition built up in the villages. Many young people were at first reluctant to leave the security of their extended families in the friendly if overcrowded comfort of the old villages, where community was well established.

The villagers of Hetton described 'Farewell to Squalor' as 'Clarkes Mein Kampf', and declared that:

' as free people the residents of South Hetton wish to make it clear that, without any bravado, they were not going to Peterlee. If the Minister was not to permit new houses in South Hetton then the people would prefer to remain in their slums rather than live in a place to which they had been compulsorily removed'

By 1955 the population of Peterlee had risen to 6,000, 1,500 short of its target, but by 1960 there was a waiting list of over 2,000. The population of Peterlee at this time consisted mainly of young couples with young families, reflecting the fact that the practice of living in for the first years of marriage was on the decline. In the end, if an alternative was provided the benefits of on-the-spot childminders were outweighed by the advantages of space and privacy. In the absence of new housing stock in the villages the only alternative was the new town.

To meet the needs of a rapidly changing mining industry a new mining college was built. After the heavy investment in the mining industry, mining was becoming a much more modern, technology-oriented business. Where the pit mechanic had once been a member of a small elite, mechanics were now one-third of the workforce, and were placed alongside the men underground. The modern apprenticeships require a year's attendance at college and then a day-release program for a further three years. The days when deputies would have worked their way up over decades through the various classes of workmen, educating themselves in their own time to take their deputy's tickets, was over. Future managers were now to be chosen at 16 and modern mining apprentices were trained as much in the classroom as down the pit.

Wheatley Hill colliery

Thornley colliery

By the mid-60's cheap oil was pouring into the country in ever-increasing quantities and nuclear energy was hailed as the fuel of the future.

In 1965 the National Union of Mineworkers made a Faustian pact with the Labour Government. The Government agreed to write off the £415 million debt which the industry had accrued in compensating the former owners and modernising the super-pits if the union agreed not to oppose the closure of the unprofitable units. Pits throughout the coalfields began to close at the rate of one a week.

To the West of the county the collieries were going down like ninepins and in the East Wingate, Wheatley Hill and Thornley were all to close before the decade was out. Many families migrated from these villages to more secure jobs in Nottinghamshire, Leicestershire, Yorkshire, Staffordshire and even as far as South Wales.

And yet confidence in the long-term future of the super-pits on the coast was high. Off-shore boring throughout the decade revealed massive reserves of coal, sufficient, according to NCB Chairman Alf Robens, to secure the life of the coastal collieries for 100 years. The discovery of millions of tons of reserves alongside the Government's decision to build a nuclear power station on the southern end of the coalfield in sight of the pits seemed an ominous contradiction.

Nichol Chapman leading Murton band and banner, Durham Miners Gala circa, 1950s

Chapter 6

Blackhall banner at Durham Miners' Gala 1970s

The years of co-operation between the miners union and the Government had taken their toll, and by the end of the 1960s miners had slipped down the earnings league. The National Power-loading agreement, signed in 1966, had replaced piece work at nearly all collieries, and while Durham's rates were below those of other coalfield areas wages for the first time since 1912 became a powerful grievance uniting all miners.

Barry Chambers became interested in the union in 1968 when he was working in extremely wet conditions at Blackhall colliery. He and his working 'marras' approached the union to be paid excessive wet money and after much persistence they achieved a payment of five shillings a shift and were allowed to finish a half-hour before their time. He stood for the union committee in 1968 and failed to get a position but the following year he was successful.

Grumbling Discontent

That year the grumbling discontent on the wages question began to emerge when the Yorkshire Area came out on unofficial strike and appealed for support in Durham. Easington, Vane Tempest and Dawdon supported them by taking strike action.

Barry remembered:

'When Dawdon and Easington came out in support of the Yorkshire surface workers in 1969 we had gone down the pit on back-shift. When we got underground we heard that the Easington lads had landed at the pit to picket us out but had arrived too late. They thought that our back shift was half-past-nine. So we decided to come out-bye. When we got to the surface we heard that other seams were coming out-bye.

When we got to bank I was told by the Lodge Officials that with me being on the committee

I should have known better. Then the Financial Secretary arrived and he agreed with me that we should be on strike. We wanted to call a special meeting there and then but all kinds of excuses were given why we could not have it at five o' clock that day. By this time we were still arguing and it was one o' clock in the morning. In the end the management agreed to let the first-shift men ride sharp so they could attend a meeting the next morning.

'We had the meeting and three resolutions were put: to strike, not to strike or to have an overtime ban. To my everlasting disappointment the overtime ban was passed. Looking back, for Blackhall at that time, it was quite a good outcome.

'I later found out that Horden was standing by waiting to see what Blackhall was going to do, which was the wrong way round. A pit the size of Horden should not have been waiting to see what we were going to do.'

Barry explained the background to the strike of 1972:

'The reason for the 1972 strike was that the power-loading wage had sunk to such a level that I used to hear even the moderate older men say, " Well young'un dint worry about the pit — you can work anywhere for nowt". Prior to that period you always had that attitude which said "nowt was ever gained by strikes", By 1971-72 that had gone. When I first started the pit their were a lot of men like that and they were looked upon as godfathers. Men would say they are the men who have gone through it and they know what they are talking about.

'And then there were all these reports of how far we had dropped down the wages league. But we knew ourselves. A man could fall off on the sick towards the end of the tax year and with the bit tax rebate he got he was actually getting more money than if he was working'.

The Miners Strike Back

The defeats of the 20s and 30s were now a distant memory in the minds of the older men. A younger and more confident workforce voted to strike, the first national action of the miners union since 1926. The government of Ted Heath was caught on the hop. The country had long taken for granted the compliance of the NUM. The Government was not prepared and coal stocks were low.

Barry Chambers knew the miners were winning when he experienced the first power cut.

'During the strike there were plenty of people telling us we were going to have no pits to go back to. They would say they are wanting to close the pits and you are going to do it for them.

'I can always remember during the strike I had been down to Hartlepool to see the pickets and we were driving back passed the West View estate and all of a sudden it went black. There had hardly been a mention that coal stocks were getting low and that there would be power cuts. Then all of a sudden bang the lights went out and I said we've done it! I never thought it would be as soon as that.

'Then we had the Wilberforce enquiry and I'll never forget the night the Executive Committee were meeting to decide whether they were going to accept the Wilberforce recommendation.

'We were all in the Hardwick public house and we all thought we had won. Then in comes Henry Smith, one of those old miners the kind that still chew baccy in the club, and he says "Whad y' think them Communist bastards on the Executive Committee have gone and done. They've just gone and turned the Wilberforce award down!"

'"O have they?", I said.

'He kept on flinging his arms around and shouting "They've turned Wilberforce down. They're just bloody Communists that's all they are!"

'A ripple of discontent started to run round the room and some men were saying, "That's bloody ridiculous, that's bloody ridiculous!".

'"Bear with them", I said, "Just bear with them, them lads know what they're doing. They've taken us this far".

'"Get away to hell!", one man shouted. "I'm bloody hard up I want to get back to work!"

'Well, before the session ended at ten o clock it came over on the news:

'" The miners Executive have accepted a

further seven rest days to settle the national dispute'".

'I went straight across to Henry Smith and I said, "Lucker, its taken the National Executive two hours to get that extra weeks holiday we've been fighting for 20 years". Well if you could have seen his face!

'Mind, I was glad it only took two hours 'cos I wouldn't have liked to have taken the flak for a full weekend'.

Horden 1976

Engine 'Gamma' at Vane Tempest colliery,1974

Miners received a £5.00 increase in the power-loading rate of pay and an extra 7 rest days. Conditions had improved but the threat to the inland pits continued and on September 2 1972 Shotton colliery was closed and the labour force was transferred to the surrounding collieries.

The NCB however seemed heavily committed to the coastal collieries and on March 23 1973 approval was given to Dawdon and Vane Tempest to embark on a huge development of reserves in the North Sea. Later that year the NCB announced that Horden and Blackhall collieries were to be linked in a scheme which was to cost £5.5M.

The fortunes of coal were changing. The Middle East crisis of 1973 was to see the price of oil triple. Coal, which had suffered so long as a result of cheap oil now looked an attractive proposition.

In November 1973 the NUM, keen to take advantage of the situation and restore miners' wages to their rightful position in the earnings league, embarked on an overtime ban. Immediately the Heath government declared a State of Emergency and made a revised pay offer which was rejected. By December 14 Heath was desperate and in a broadcast to the nation announced a three-day week for industry to conserve coal stocks.

1974 Ballot

On February 4 1974 a national ballot of NUM members produced an 80.99 per cent majority for strike action, Durham voting 85.7 per cent in favour. Times were changing and Durham's post-war reputation as a moderate area now looked out of date.

In response Heath called a General Election on the slogan: who rules the country, the government or the unions? The miners refused to call off the strike and on February 28 1974 the Labour Party emerged from the General Election as the largest single party, holding 301 seats to the Tories 296. Heath was reluctant to leave Downing Street and on March 4 he met with Jeremy Thorpe, leader of the Liberal Party, to get his support to form an administration. He failed, and for the third time the Labour Party formed a minority government. Miners achieved their full wages demand, an extra payment for shift working, £30 in lieu of a weeks holiday that year and a further week's holiday from 1975.

Second Plan for Coal

Almost immediately the government instituted a second Plan for Coal and ushered in another era of co-operation which was to see the decade out.

On March 14 1974 Derek Ezra visited the area to

announce a £5M investment in Easington colliery to develop the under-sea reserves.

Eric Varley the new Minister for Energy, told the NUM executive:

' King Coal was back on his throne again... No one can knock him off . The only way he can lose is by abdication'.

In 1974 the NCB lost no time in attempting to introduce an incentive scheme that would ensure that once again miners would be divided by the level of their earnings. The miners rejected their advances in a coalfield ballot but the NCB and their supporters in the union were persistent and continued to advocate the introduction of an incentive scheme.

A national incentive scheme based on the total production of all collieries was agreed but this was far from the more individualised scheme that the Coal Board required and was short-lived.

In 1976 after a brief wrangle over terms a new pensions scheme was introduced which was to become the richest in the country. An agreement followed to bring down the age of retirement in stages from 65 to 60 for all miners who had over 20 years underground service.

In 1977 proposals for an incentive scheme were again rejected by National Conference and by a coalfield ballot. Still the supporters of the incentive scheme continued to fight for its introduction.

The most enthusiastic advocates were the leaders of the Nottingham and South Derbyshire Areas. Since the formation of the National Union of Mineworkers the union had never become a truly national union and remained a federation of autonomous area unions. Consequently the leaders in Nottingham and South Derbyshire were able to argue that they could introduce area incentive schemes even though a national scheme had been rejected twice in a national ballot.

When later that year area incentive schemes were introduced in Nottingham and South Derbyshire an orchestrated campaign within the union and throughout the media made much of the generous bonuses that were being earned by miners in these two counties. Miners' leaders in the areas adhering to national policy then experienced intense pressure from members who thought that they were missing out on extra earnings. The result was predictable and within a few months practically all areas had introduced incentive schemes with such haste that the finer important details were overlooked.

No one knew at this time that the introduction of

an incentive scheme was the major proposal in the Miron Report — a secret report drawn up by Wilfred Miron, a member of the Coal Board. The Miron report was a long-term strategy to destroy the power of the NUM.

In 1978, Nicholas Ridley, a close confidant of Margaret Thatcher, drew up a further strategy to defeat the NUM. This strategy involved the creation of mobile police squads organised on national lines, the encouragement of non-union haulage companies to transport coal, rigging the energy market in favour of nuclear energy, building up coal stocks and the introduction of duel oil /coal-burning power stations.

The latter half of the 1970s saw a lull in the pace of pit closures and the East coast collieries seemed as secure as they had been for 70 years — despite a few warning shots which had threatened Vane Tempest.

There were also some disappointments. Dawdon and Vane Tempest collieries in a joint operation struck east to reach the newly proven reserves under the North Sea. As the roadways pushed eastwards the seams crept closer and closer to the permian until they were too close to be safe. The discovery of these antipodes - dome shaped distortions in the seams - was a big blow to the long term life of the two collieries but not immediately life-threatening.

The NCB declared that the reserves could still be worked from Easington's workings by going behind the antipodes.

The only coastal colliery that was looking vulnerable as the decade drew to a close was Blackhall in the extreme south of the coalfield. Barry Chambers explained why this was so:

> It was the close proximity of our workings to the permian strata that led to all the water problems at Blackhall. We couldn't work the High Main at Blackhall for that reason whereas at Horden they were working it right up to the end.
>
> In the 1940s they were working the South Low Main under Hartlepool Golf course when they realised they were only 30 ft from the sand feed so they got to hell out of it as sharp as possible. They sent car loads of stone in to pack it up so it didn't all come away and flood the pit.
>
> Blackhall was on the edge of the workable coalfield and too close to the permian and the water. This was the pit's downfall towards the end.
>
> We were taking a 60 yard strip of coal out and having to leave a 60 yard strip to hold the roof up. Later we were leaving a hundred yard

strip. Well you can imagine the amount of development work require to keep that up. Every where you went there was a Dosco or a Dintheader.

There was always a problem with the water at Blackhall. Whenever the electricity was off for any length of time you would end up with a Dosco being flooded out. As soon as the electricity was off you had to start pulling the Doscos back to higher ground.

Then the coal started to thin out and was less

than a yard high. With these conditions we had a high turnover of labour. I've known times when after the pit holidays up to 60 men would 'rap in' and not come back. So when collieries closed in other parts of the coalfield the transferred men were usually sent to Blackhall.

When people say you never tried to keep the pit open.... if they only knew the problem we were having to put up with'.

When the pit closed on April 6 1981 few people

Blackhall colliery

were surprised and few complained. The men who wanted to remain in the industry were transferred to neighbouring collieries.

The amount of water now pouring into Blackhall workings was so great that if left it would have inundated the surrounding collieries. The colliery was therefore kept open as a pumping station, the cost of which was now a further burden on the remaining collieries.

The 1970s ended on a pessimistic note for the miners of the East coast collieries. On May 1979 the Tory Party was restored to office under the leadership of Margaret Thatcher, who lost no time in telling the NCB that it must make a profit. A government Bill was passed in April 1980 requiring the NCB to make a profit by the 1984.

In 1981 there was a warning of things to come when Derek Ezra, the chairman of the NCB, announced the closure of 32 collieries throughout the country, four of them in County Durham. These four Durham pits, Sacriston, Boldon, Houghton and Bearpark took immediate strike action alongside the other threatened collieries throughout the country, and a national ballot was called. The new Tory government was not prepared for an all out-strike and the closure notices were withdrawn and a subsidy was awarded to the NCB to set against its losses.

Arthur Scargill

On December 6 1981 Arthur Scargill was elected as leader of the National Union of Mineworkers with a massive majority of 70.3 per cent. With Margaret Thatcher in 10 Downing Street and Arthur Scargill leading the NUM many speculated that a confrontation was in the offing.

However the miners balloted in 1982 and 1983 not to take action on wages and pit closures and it looked as if a confrontation was to be avoided.

When in September 1983 the Thatcher government appointed Ian MacGregor, an American industrialist with a reputation of butchering jobs, to replace Derek Ezra as the Chairman of the NCB fears were renewed that the government was seeking a conflict with the NUM.

SEAM Campaign

Despite the run-down of labour in the mining industry which had now continued for 70 years there were still 12,000 miners in the Easington area and few new industries had been attracted to the area to replace coal as the centre of the local economy.

For the first time the realisation grew amongst the local branches of the NUM in the Easington area that the super-pits of East Durham were now under threat. To counter this threat the local Labour Party called all the local unions and community groups to a meeting on Friday December 16 1983 at Easington District offices to set up a campaigning organisation to fight the threat posed by MacGregor.

The organisation set up at this meeting was called Save Easington Area Mines (SEAM). Their aim was to mobilise the whole community to oppose the closure of the mines. Heather Wood, the daughter of an Easington miner was elected chair person and Alan Barker, an Easington miner was elected secretary. Throughout the winter of 83/84 the campaign met regularly inviting expert speakers from the mining and power-generation industries.

Children were encouraged to be involved and a poster competition was organised in the local schools. Many of the posters reflected a deeply felt sense of history that was shared across the generations in a community dependent upon the production of coal.

The SEAM campaign called a demonstration in Easington on February 26 1984 inviting Neil Kinnock, the leader of the Labour Party as the main speaker. Bands and banners from across the

Women and children of the SEAM Campaign
Photo: Keith Pattison

county turned out and the vast hall of the Easington Miners' Welfare was packed for the rally. At the head of the demonstration was the banner of Polmaise colliery in Scotland. Polmaise colliery had been on strike for a week after the NCB had announced the closure of the colliery.

On March 6 the Yorkshire Area took strike action after the closure of Cortonwood colliery. Cortonwood, unlike Polmaise was not a colliery with a particularly militant history, but it was to be the closure of this colliery which would go down in history as the spark which ignited the 1984/85 conflagration.

On March 12 a Special Coalfield Conference of Durham miners called all Durham pits to take strike action against the threat of pit closures, and by March 14 all Durham pits were idle.

Within two weeks all the coalfields in Britain were on strike with the exception of Nottinghamshire, South Derbyshire and Leicestershire.

Despite many reservations voiced in the first weeks of the strike Durham and its East coast collieries, true to their traditions, remained loyal to the National Union and set about the task of winning the strike. Central to this task were the community's women.

Women Get Organised

In the weeks before the strike the SEAM campaign had been calling for more women to join the organisation and for this purpose had called a meeting specifically for women. The strike was not two weeks old when this meeting took place, and in a packed council chamber at the Easington Council offices they set about the organisation of feeding centres.

Heather Wood, the chairperson, insisted that these feeding centres would not be called 'soup kitchens', a name which evoked the defeats of the 20s and the depression of the 30s. These centres were to be called 'Miners Cafes'. The first in the county was opened in the Colliery Club, Easington and the first food was provided by a food co-operative in Durham. Within weeks 13 cafes had been established throughout the Easington area.

Local shops and businesses made regular contributions. In Murton the local shoe shop donated a pair of shoes each week to a child of a miner. Most but not all business were as generous. One butcher in Murton refused to give anything and was repaid by the community in equal measure. What little miners and their families had was not spent in that shop and by the end of the strike the butcher was out of business.

In an area where the major portion of the work-force was out of work the problem of raising sufficient resources was a constant one. At that

SEAM kitchen in Colliery Club Easington 1984   *Photo: Keith Pattison*

time within the North-East area there were 24,000 miners on strike in the counties of Northumberland and Durham. With a total population of a little over 3 million in only three major centres of population, collecting food to feed the families was a major task. It was obvious that many of the resources would have to come from outside the area. To help overcome this problem the Labour Council of Greenwich twinned with Easington to support the community.

During the course of the strike miners and their families were regular visitors to Greenwich, where they were received generously by a quite different multi-ethnic community.

While the two communities differed in their social composition they were united in a common desire to help the miners and their families survive the year.

For five months Durham remained totally solid

Easington colliery, October 1984   *Photo Keith Pattison*

and its miners were drafted to other areas where the communities were split between working and striking miners. From the first days of the strike the government organised a massive police operation to prevent striking miners coming into contact with working miners. The right to travel freely was suspended, at least for miners. Villages were occupied by huge contingents of police drafted from all regions of the country.

On several occasions the NCB offered inducements for men to return to work but to no effect. In August the NCB was able to induce a miner from the West of the county to return to work at Easington colliery. The community of Easington was regarded as one of the most solid in the county and the local manager had given a guarantee to the local miners' lodge that if a miner returned to work against the wishes of the NUM then he would have to walk under his own steam through the main gates of the colliery. In the fullness of time such local guarantees were proved worthless and in the presence of thousands of police officers drawn from far away as Gwent in Wales and Leicestershire a solitary strikebreaker sneaked in through the back door of the colliery on Friday August 24.

Easington colliery, October 1984   *Photo Keith Pattison*

Five months on strike without wages, the violation of civil rights, and systematic police violence exploded into uncontrollable rage. A riot ensued in the course of which damage was done to the colliery yard, the offices and the colliery officials' cars. Next morning the roads into Easington colliery were blocked by the police and no miner was allowed to enter.

The East Durham area was now in a state of siege. On the night of the Easington disturbance riot police amassed on the outskirts of the village of Murton just as the pubs were due to close. Murton like Easington was regarded as one of the most solid areas of the strike. In all conflicts perception of truth is often determined by which side of the dispute the observer is on. The police said they entered the village after a disturbance was reported. The miners say the police entered the village and provoked a riot.

Cars were pulled across the road in front of the Colliery Inn, and the Travellers Rest which had already suffered fire damage was again set on fire. Residents reported that their front doors were kicked down by members of the riot squad in pursuit of miners.

The result of the incident was that several Murton miners were sent to prison for periods up to 18 Months and were subsequently sacked by the NCB. Men from Dawdon and Easington were jailed after other incidents.

These events marked a decisive turning-point in the strike but it was not until six months later, after one year on strike, that the miners of East Durham and their comrades across the county marched defiantly

Easington under siege   *Photo: Keith Pattison*

Murton miners return to work   Photo: John Adie

in their thousands, behind their lodge banners, brass bands playing, into the pit yards. All lodges in respect for the women in the community, whose efforts could never be rewarded, asked the women's support groups to carry the lodge banners.

1984 / 85 was a defining moment in the history of East Durham. The mining community had endured its longest and most bitter strike. Subsequent revelations would demonstrate that they had come tantalisingly close to victory. They had not won a guarantee that the pits would remain open but if Thatcher's aim had been to destroy the NUM then she had not achieved a victory either. Experience was to prove in the years ahead that the dragon had not been slain and the union was still able to fight for its members.

The Durham Area NUM was to change in the aftermath of the strike when in 1986 David Guy, the former treasurer of Dawdon lodge, was elected to the post of Area President and David Hopper, the former secretary of Wearmouth Lodge was elected General Secretary. Just prior to the strike Bill Etherington, secretary of Dawdon Mechanics, had been elected as General Secretary of the Durham Colliery Mechanics Association. The election of these three Area Officials represented a shift to the left in the politics of Durham miners.

Once the dispute was over MacGregor's revenge was swift, and in East Durham he turned his attention to Horden colliery.

In the years prior to the strike Horden had inherited the water problems of Blackhall. Throughout the strike the Horden miners' lodge had provided safety cover to prevent the colliery from flooding. To allow the colliery to flood would, they argued, have played into the hands of the NCB.

The union at Horden colliery had been unhappy for some time due to a decision taken by the NCB as far back as 1973 to allow Easington colliery to develop the J seam in zone 6 of Horden's take without consultation with the union. The dispute came to a head in 1981 when the NCB decided that the E seam in zone 6 was too close to the permian water to be mined by Horden. Faces had already been developed in this seam and it was calculated that faces could not be developed in the G seam until 1983.

The board argued that in 1980 zone 5 of Easington's reserves had been seeded to Horden and although Easington had found difficulties in mining this zone the prospects from the Horden side looked good.

The colliery was losing money, due in no small part to the £3.5 m cost per year of pumping water out of the mine. The management proposed a plan to reduce manpower from 1,700 to 1,200 and to achieve a target of 3,000 tons of coal raised per day. The unions reluctantly accepted this plan as the best way of securing a future for the colliery.

Within months of the end of the strike the future of Horden colliery was in danger. The tactics of the NCB, now called British Coal, were to become well known across the coalfield. Firstly they allowed a run-down of labour by allowing men to take redundancy. They then reduced the number of faces to two.

By reducing the number of faces they placed all the eggs in one or two baskets. If those faces hit problems then there would be no spare capacity with which to retrieve the situation. The Report entitled '(Mis) Managing Horden', produced by the Employment Research Unit of Durham University, quoted the NUM lodge secretary Ervine Lyons as saying that,

> 'the pit has been pinned back. It's like a vice they've put us in. Were a big pit, now we're down to two faces. Every way the Board has pushed us back'.

When finally the closure of the pit was announced the unions appealed to the men not to seek redundancy or transfer and to take the pit through the Modified Review Procedure.

The women's support groups called a rally in Horden in support of the fight to keep the colliery open. The men in the main remained loyal to the union and the pit was taken through the Modified Review Procedure.

The Colliery Review Procedure had been modified in an attempt to prevent the Deputies Union NACODS joining the 1984 / 85 strike in October 1984. The deputies had voted by a massive majority to join the strike but the

Seaham miners meet to discuss fighting closure   Photo: Stan Gamester

leadership accepted the modified procedure, which made provision for independent arbitrators selected by the unions and the NCB to preside over the review. Their decision was, however, not to be binding on the NCB, who would only have to place 'due weight' on the decision of the Review.

One of the main arguments of the NUM against the closure of Horden was the effect that closure of the colliery would have on the East Durham area, already suffering a high level of unemployment due to the economy being so heavily dependent on coal. The NUM called this the 'social cost' and was able to prove that this 'social cost' was greater than the projected losses of Horden colliery.

The lack of enthusiasm of successive governments to bring industry into the area which would compete with the manpower requirements of the NCB in the East Durham area had left a legacy.

'(Mis) Managing Horden' quoted a miner who said:

> 'There's more people living off the dead carcass of a pit like Blackhall than in most advanced factories. In pay terms you need to create two jobs to replace one lost mining job. I can't see anybody who could replace 2000 lost mining jobs in Blackhall'.

Horden lost its fight in the review procedure and was closed in February 1986. Horden set a pattern for the closure program. So long as the 'social cost' of closure was ruled as 'inadmissible evidence' in the colliery Review Procedure, all that British Coal had to demonstrate was that the colliery was not making a profit.

Seaham colliery was closed after a review in the same year.

Murton miners celebrate achieving the fastest million tons 1987

The union complained that British Coal's strategy rested on a psychological war to convince men to leave the industry. Large redundancy payments were offered but only for specific periods. As the cut-off date approached rumours circulated that this would be the last payment and if there was another scheme then the terms would be worse than those on offer.

As more left the industry the conditions underground deteriorated as production intensified. The maintenance of roadways and belt lines was neglected. Overtime working on the coal face, once hardly known in many pits, became commonplace. The result was a general wearing down of resolve and the belief that anything, even the prospect of long term unemployment, was better than working under these conditions.

In December 1988 British Coal announced that at Dawdon colliery there were no workable reserves left in the E 90 area of the pit. The proposed development in G80 and G81 was below a huge pond of water that had been discovered, containing an estimated 11 million gallons of water. In the interests of safety management announced that they were to abandon one million tons of coal in this area.

A plan to work the 3.8m tons of reserves in C seam at the rate of 4,000 tons of coal per day and employing 1,000 men for four years was reluctantly accepted by the men. In the event thinning of the C seam shortened this prediction and the colliery closed in July 1991.

Rally against the closure of Murton colliery October 1991
Photo: Stan Gamester

Vane Tempest colliey 1991

It was now five years since the end of the year-long strike and the pace of closures throughout the country was accelerating. The promise that 'due weight' would be given to the review procedure was seen for what it was when British Coal lost its case for the closure of Bates colliery in Northumberland. The colliery was closed in defiance of the review decision.

British Coal now saw the Review Procedure as an impediment to the swift closure of the colliery. The three months to exhaust the procedure only cost money and time.

Off to London

Ariving in London

Photos: Stan Gamester

Vane Tempest miners maching in London against pit closures October 1992

By the end of 1991 there were only three collieries left in East Durham. Vane Tempest, Easington and Murton. Murton was to be the next target.

British Coal's tactics were familiar. The number of districts worked was reduced until the targeted output of 4,000 tons per day was dependent on only two faces. When one of these faces, E78b, hit bad roof conditions it was closed down. The colliery had been put in the Review Procedure some months before and all the unions at the pit united in the local Miners Federation to oppose the closure. They were successful in persuading all of the workforce to resist the temptation of taking redundancy and even when special interviews were organised with the men, all to a man refused to ask for redundancy.

Faced with this degree of unity British Coal announced that the pit would stop coal work and every one working at the colliery on power-loading would be downgraded to the datal rate of pay. Since there would be no production then no production bonus would be paid. Since redundancy payments were based on the wages being earned at the time of redundancy then the men would lose thousands.

The alternative offered by British Coal was for the men to vote to withdraw the colliery from the Review Procedure . If they did there would be no downgrading and British Coal would pay a massive £100 bonus per week until closure. This effectively meant that everyone at the colliery would receive the maximum redundancy payment. The union stood by its principle of always exhausting the review procedure but not unexpectedly the men chose to take the offer of transfer or the enhanced redundancy payments.

East Durham was now down to two collieries, Vane Tempest and Easington.

In October 1992 Heseltine made his now notorious announcement that 32 collieries would close without a guarantee that men who wished to stay in the industry would be offered a job at other collieries. At the same time he announced that the Modified Colliery Review Procedure was to be suspended. There was an enormous outcry from the general public and within a week, on October 21, an estimated 250,000 people marched through the streets of London in protest. Campaign headquarters were set up at the miners' office in Red Hill and every available train and bus was hired to transport people to the demonstration. Hundreds of thousands of pounds were collected by supporters for a fighting fund.

On the following Sunday even more people came out to support the miners in a second massive demonstration in London. It appeared that the whole country was up in arms and in the following weeks demonstrations took place in every major centre of population.

The NUM held a ballot and embarked on a series of one-day stoppages against the closures. British Coal tried to undermine the action by making exaggerated claims of how much redundancy money would be lost by those who took action against the closures.

The miners' union proceeded to seek injunctions against the closure of collieries. British Coal countered this legal approach by offering the maximum payment of redundancy across the board at all the mines where the men agreed to withdraw from the legal challenge. The men at Easington colliery accepted this offer and the colliery closed in May 1993. Vane Tempest men refused to withdraw their legal challenge. They fought on and lost both the legal challenge and the extra redundancy money. Some men lost up to £7,000 and despite further legal battles have been unable to recoup their losses.

Coalmining in East Durham which had sustained the people for almost two centuries was now at an end. The battle for coal under the limestone began with a battle against the water in the sand feeder. The struggle to keep the water at bay never ended but in the end it was not the water that closed the mines but a short-term economic policy.

History did not begin with coal mines and nor did it end when they were destroyed. The indomitable spirit and the character of mining communities was fashioned in the hard and often brutal battle to wrest coal from nature, and in determined resistance to exploitation. That spirit will endure: and men and women will tackle new problems and rise to new challenges. Pits close, but people live on and fight. Some will say, 'things will never be the same as they used to be'.... But they never are and they never were.

Banners of Easington District

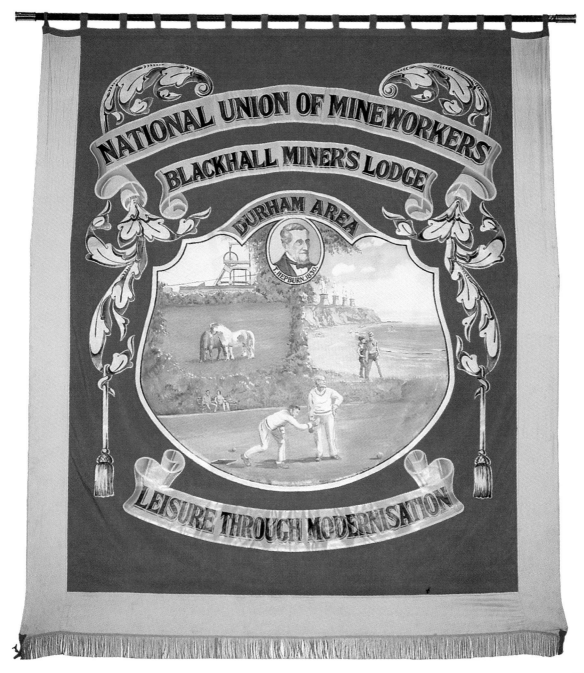

NATIONAL UNION OF MINEWORKERS

BLACKHALL MINER'S LODGE

DURHAM AREA

T. HEPBURN, 1830.

LEISURE THROUGH MODERNISATION

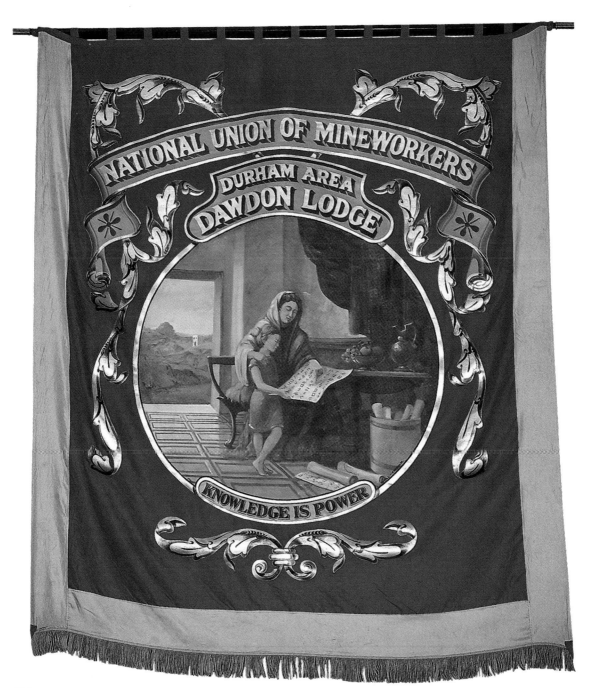

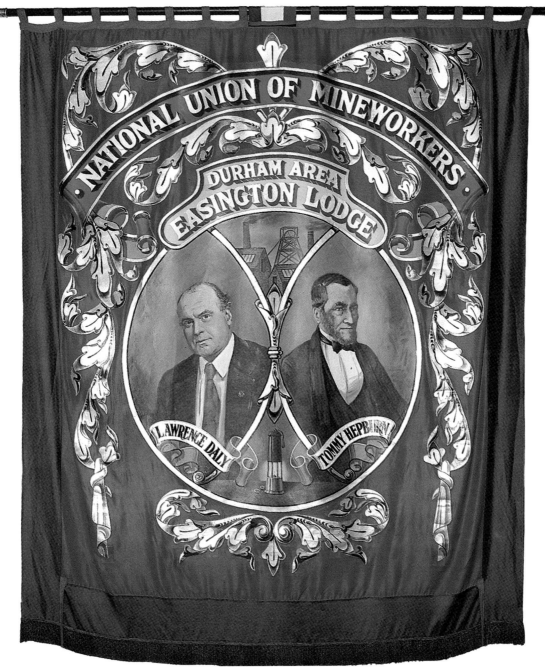

·NATIONAL UNION OF MINEWORKERS·

DURHAM AREA
EASINGTON LODGE

"WE REMEMBER"

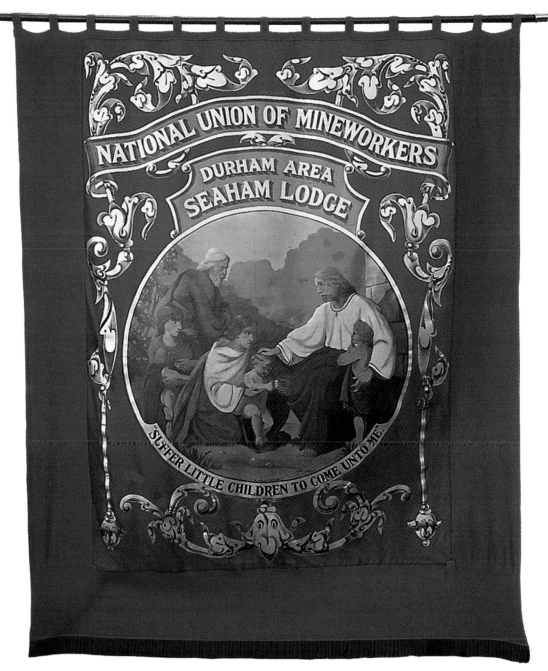

Easington District — the Past in Pictures

Colliery Blacksmiths, Murton ,1885

Murton Territorials, 1900

Old peoples outing, Murton, 1900

Commercial Street, Wingate, circa 1900

Murton Rapper Sword Dance Team, circa 1904

Members of Wingate Chapel Choir, circa 1900

Marlborough Street, Seaham, 1907

Wingate quarry football club, 1912-13

Blackhills Terrace, Horden 1913

New Seaham Store staff, circa 1915

Seaham lifeboat, 1911

Church Street, Seaham Harbour, circa 1915

Local boxers, Seaham, 1920. Front row from left: Reece Hope, Billy Hardy.
Back row left: Murphy

Murton miners, 1920

Wesleyan Chapel concert, Seaham, circa 1920

Dawdon Colliery Girls' school, 1921

Opening ceremony of Thornley colliery scheme house, Dunelm Road South, 24 August 1924

South Hetton pit lads, circa 1929

Building the Coast Road, 1923-24

Rock House garden party, Seaham, circa 1930

Groom and horse at hospital carnival, Easington RDC, 1930

Lodge officials, Vane Tempest, with first banner, 1931

Trimdon miners, Back row left to right: Tommy Souby, William Harper Snr., J. Kell
Front row left to right: Dicky Harper and Billy Harper

Horden Labour Club committee men, circa 1930

Group of Murton men

Metcalf's Store, 1935

Deaf Hill Welfare Band

AJ Dawson Grammar School, Welfield, circa, 1937

Horden beach post card, circa 1930

It's Glorious
on the Beach at
HORDEN

THE CLIFFS, BLACKHALL ROCKS.

Andrew sisters, Butcher Street, 1948

Seaham and district miners at convalescent home, 1940

Colliery garages, Blackhall, 1940s

Leek show, Horden Workingmens Club, 1945

Mr Smart and son, showing pit ponies Wolf and Sterling, 1958

Murton Athletic club, 1953

Members of Murton weightlifting club, 1960